OVER THE WALL

The Men Behind the 1934 Death House Escape

Best Wishes —

" They always go home..."

Patrick McConal

Patrick M. McConal

11/9/00

EAKIN PRESS ◁Ṽ▷ Austin, Texas

Library of Congress Cataloging-in-Publication Data

McConal, Patrick M.
    Over the wall : the men behind the 1934 death house escape / by Patrick M.
McConal.
        p.   cm.
    Includes bibliographical references and index.
    ISBN 1-57168-365-8
    1. Walker, Whitey. Criminals—United States—Biography. Death row inmates—
Texas—Huntsville—Biography. Escapes—Texas—Huntsville—Case studies.
HV6245   .M2322   2000
365/.641   21

Cover art by Stuart Thompson

To my wife, Pamela.
Happy twentieth anniversary.

Contents

Acknowledgments

I apologize up front to all the individuals who have helped me in this enormous project whom I have forgotten to mention. People from all across the United States helped me gather information to attempt to piece this puzzle together. I want to especially thank several people for their efforts and contributions.

This project began when I read an article about a local robbery and kidnapping that took place in 1933. The robbery interested me because it was yet another example of a crime that Bonnie and Clyde were accused of but didn't commit—the real perpetrators were the Whitey Walker Gang. That's when my research began in earnest. I needed a topic for a graduate paper at Sam Houston State University, and when I obtained some files buried in a waterlogged box in a courthouse basement, there was no turning back. This book is the result.

George Weir led a quest for me in obtaining records and performed endless footwork. He drove county clerks crazy with never taking no for an answer, and he helped me with some ideas on how to proceed. I would also like to thank author John Neal Phillips, who not only wrote what I consider the bible of all Bonnie and Clyde books, but who was also instrumental in the direction of this book. Warden Jim Willett discovered many secrets and discrepancies about the Walls Prison in Huntsville, and through many hours of digging through archived photos and examining the physical layout, his efforts have allowed the facts to overshadow many untruths written in past publications about the Walls Unit. Eloise Lane has been my eyes and ears on events relating to this subject in the Texas Panhandle. Her efforts in searching microfilmed newspaper articles, conducting interviews, gathering photos, and keeping me up-to-date saved weeks of research on my part.

Dr. Mitch Roth, my mentor at the Sam Houston State University Graduate History Department, shadowed my work so that I wouldn't stumble in the usual pitfalls of writing and research. All of the county clerks deserve recognition for going far beyond their job duties to make my source documents available. This was also true of the staff of the Texas State Archives in Austin. Jessica Franklin typed my chicken scratch and transcribed my recorded ramblings to meet unreasonable deadlines.

Martha Palmer is the reason the book expanded in scope to include her uncle, Joe Palmer of the Barrow Gang, and I would not have found her without the support of Partners in Crime, an Internet research support group of which I am a member. Hugh Kennedy is responsible for smuggling out of prison the photos taken by him at the places where these events occurred, as well as offering his account as an eyewitness at the Eastham Raid.

From the Texas Department of Criminal Justice, I would like to thank Terry Wunderlich, Simon Beardsley, and Wendy Ingram for their assistance in compiling prison records critical to this book. I would also like to thank Major David Bone and Warden Jimmy Alford for going out of their way to provide visual inspections and background information regarding the Eastham State Farm. Larry Fitzgerald was the contact who enabled me to create the network that made everything on the prison side come together. Jan Henley of Madisonville, Texas, was responsible for the contacts in the chapter, "Rabbit Runs at Eastham."

Last-minute windfalls of information and photos of the Whitey Walker Gang came from W. J. Ford, Sandra Walker, Roy Walker, and Janet Johnson. Others who led to vital bank robbery and kidnapping information were Richard Crow and Anne Davidson. Clara Mounce of the Bryan Public Library discovered the missing file folder that revealed many facts of the Caldwell Jewelry Robbery, as well as provided photos for this book. The curator of the Mobeetie Museum, Louise Hogan, and the county attorney of Wheeler led me to missing facts regarding Blackie Thompson.

Kelly West, Leslie Pourteau, and Stuart Thompson were the copy and graphics editing group who made this book ready for submission. Technical support, endnotes, and copy editing were the product of Michelle Walker.

I would like to thank Mrs. Violet Dolehite of Rogers, Texas, for taking me through the woods to find an abandoned road that was the spot of the Marlin kidnapping; she guided me through those woods when she was over eighty years of age. An article written by Judge Tom McDonald Jr. about the Whitey Walker Gang brought this story to life.

Jonathan Davis was the historical specialist from Dallas who kept my facts in check. My father, Jon McConal, made me stay on track, and fortunately he read the first draft and made corrections before I buried myself under flaws in the book.

Richard Farris of Palestine rolled out the red carpet for me to get what I needed there.

I would like to thank Ed Eakin for taking the chance to publish something that many people have wanted to see come to light. I thank my children, Morgan, Maegan, and Brady, for tolerating my fifteen-month hibernation while trying to meet my deadline.

This book was edited for final submission by Chris Pourteau.

Whitey Walker Gang
Crime Spree 1933 to 1934

Robinson Bank
Oct. 26, 1933

Marlin Bank
Dec. 27, 1933

Eastham Raid
Jan. 16, 1934

Buckholts Bank
Oct. 6, 1933

Death House Escape
July 22, 1934

Caldwell Jewelry
Dec. 14, 1933

This is a mid-1930s highway map, showing the actual roads the gang would have taken to safety.

—Map art by Stuart Thompson

They Always Go Home

It has often been said that outlaws always go back home. It was true with the James Gang, and with Bonnie and Clyde, and it would be true with the Whitey Walker Gang. Whether it was the small town of Rogers, Texas, or the oil fields of Borger in the Panhandle, the core members of the gang usually appeared to be with each other or with family.

It is not surprising, then, that when two murderers and one bank robber escaped from the Oklahoma Penitentiary at McAlester that they would head to where they could be hidden, cared for, and insulated from the law. It was the summer of 1933, and the Great Depression was as hard on the small towns as ever. Farms either went bust or were taken over by the banks. Others would simply be abandoned in the hope there was some opportunity in the bigger towns. People did the best they could, and there are countless stories of individuals and families helping strangers—their fellow men—in this time of economic collapse.

Not everyone took the high road to keep from drowning in the hard times of depression-era Texas. Whether from sheer necessity, laziness, greed, or frustration and hopelessness, some individuals followed a path of taking what they wanted in those desperate times.

This book chronicles the lives of the men who made one of the most daring prison escapes in the history of the Texas Prison System, the Death House Escape from the Walls Unit at

Huntsville. The exploits of the Whitey Walker Gang, also known as the Fishing Hole Gang, will be examined in detail for the first time, including the planning of the Huntsville escape by their leader. The men involved in this embarrassment to the Texas Prison System included some of the most desperate outlaws in the southwestern United States; for example, two members of the Barrow Gang, Joe Palmer and Raymond Hamilton. These two men were directly involved with an earlier prison escape with the help of Clyde Barrow and Bonnie Parker at the Eastham Prison Farm near Weldon, Texas. That prison break will also be discussed in detail, including the testimony of a man who was in the middle of the action that January morning in 1934.

This book is not just a here-to-there of what happened to some Texas gangsters in the years between 1933 and 1935. Although this book is a narrative of the events that took place, it also provides a glimpse of the bigger picture; it will reveal the places, the hardships, and many oral histories of individuals involved in the times. The events and people in this book are real, not some rehash of newspaper articles or fantasy reading in which everyone lives happily ever after. In this book people die. People get hurt, and people still living feel the pain of the events this book describes. The conclusion of this book propels the reader to the present, the scene of the lethal injection rather than the electric chair.

As the book progresses, the scope changes as the Whitey Walker Gang's activities grow bolder and more menacing. By that I mean that the stakes of the criminal activities grow from nickel-and-dime amounts to tens of thousands of dollars—quite a bit of money during the depression.

The lives of many outlaws involved in this turbulent period will be revealed. These people seemed to cross paths often, whether by a necessity to survive underground or by frequenting the same haunts. There will be a glimpse of their crimes, family ties, and sometimes the outlaws' feelings about their lifestyles: the *How did it come to this?* issue for these people. Although many newspapers of the period focused on Bonnie and Clyde, and the 1967 movie romanticized their misunderstood, chaotic lives, these were also the years of Joe Palmer, Ray Hamilton, Henry Methvin, Whitey Walker, Hilton Bybee, Charlie Frazier, and others. These men also made headlines and could be just as dangerous as any John Dillinger or Pretty Boy Floyd when cornered. They were all known to have good hearts, at least to their families, and their bonds with one another indicate an honor among thieves. Yet their undeniable criminal records often show vicious and murderous tendencies, sometimes against big banks, society in general, and certainly against any law enforcement authority. Whatever the causes were that brought these people to travel a self-destructive road are as important as the actions themselves. These were men who did not like to be told what to do, and they accepted the consequences for their actions. The individuals described in this book are not outlaws who rob "Ma and Pa" gas stations so that they can eat another day. These are outlaws who know what they are after and plan specifically how to get it.

On occasion there will be what a professor of mine one time called *rabbit runs*. These rabbit runs are stories not directly related to the progression of the story, but that add a special ingredient of atmosphere.

The individuals involved in the Eastham Raid and the Death House Escape were ready to do whatever was necessary to get away. And getting away doesn't just mean to escape. These people knew one way to get by in life, and that was to steal what they wanted. This is not a moral judgement. When a person escapes from the Death House, there is only one thing waiting for them if they come back to it. What it must be like for an individual in their prime in life to be sentenced to die! By the same token, what a waste of life for these young men to do what they did to deserve to die so young.

The Whitey Walker Gang did not often rob banks for huge sums of money like Dillinger or Alvin Karpis. Joe Palmer and Ray Hamilton scored even less, but they had greater notoriety in the 1930s due to their association with the Barrow Gang. All of these men had shootouts with law enforcement, but not the epic shootouts with police like Bonnie and Clyde. They do, however, show the paths of some Texans who were going to get through hard times their way. These people are bound by family ties with a rugged determinism; and they always came back home.

CHAPTER 1

Whitey Walker and the Early Years

His true name was William Jennings Bryan Walker. His headstone reads "Bryan Walker," and that is what the old-timers who knew him called him. In a sea of aliases, Bryan Walker, like so many other people in the Great Depression, used initials or nicknames. Bryan then was also "W. J.," "W. J. B.," "B. W.," "Whitey," Clyde Roberts, Walter Anderson, William Jennings Bryan, and William J. Bryan. There were others, but those are the names or aliases Bryan Walker used during his many arrests in Texas, Oklahoma, Arkansas, Colorado, and New York.

Most commonly referred to as "Whitey" Walker because of his light-colored hair, this outlaw was the son of John and Sallie Walker of Rogers, Texas. Whitey also had brothers—Hugh, Louis, and Tom. His sisters were named Ruth, Fannie, Mattie, and Kate. Dolores, or Dottie, was his wife. Later there was a second Mrs. Walker named Thula, her maiden name Hunt. It is possible either or both were marriages of convenience during crime sprees.

Born in 1897, Whitey left home at the age of eighteen. He considered himself both a farmer and a barber by occupation and had five years of formal schooling. He claimed to be a mechanical engineer at one time while being questioned for an armed bank robbery. He got his first taste of the penitentiary in

4

Oklahoma. On May 23, 1922, using the alias Clyde Roberts, he was received at the Oklahoma State Prison in McAlester as #12342 with a five-year stretch for auto theft. He was paroled, though, in less than eight months on January 3, 1923. It was Texas' turn at the young man, and at 5'10" and 140 pounds, Whitey Walker was received in the Texas State Penitentiary as inmate #52826 on May 16, 1925, for two two-year concurrent terms at the Imperial Farm for burglary and felony theft.

Governor Miriam "Ma" Ferguson was generous to the young man in granting furloughs during his incarceration due to his father's illness, as well as some mysterious problem Whitey was having with his knees. The day before Christmas in 1926, Whitey received a full pardon and was released from the Texas Prison System in Huntsville. By 1927 both Whitey and his brother Hugh Walker had moved to Borger, Texas, in the Panhandle. Borger was considered one of the roughest oil-boom towns in existence, and murder and robbery were daily events.

When not on the road or in the Texas Panhandle, Rogers, Texas, was home for Whitey. Throughout his criminal career, he still managed to go home to visit. Much like Bonnie Parker and Clyde Barrow, Whitey Walker went to great lengths as a fugitive to see his family. According to Loraine Tharp, a neighbor of the Walker family during Whitey's fugitive life, she once saw Whitey get out of a car wearing a brown dress and a bonnet to disguise himself so that he could see his mother.

Violet Dolehite, who lived two blocks from the Walker home, described the town of Rogers during the early 1920s:

> In my younger days, this town was about eight blocks. We had a motel and about seven cotton gins. But when I was about eight or nine years old, an entire block of the town burned. After that it seemed that the town just kind of went downhill. At the time that it was at its height, [it] had about four barber shops—I remember that because my father was a barber and he had a real nice shop—he had a couple of bathtubs in his shop. Men would come in on Saturday nights to take a bath and get their hair cut. He'd try to close at ten o'clock on Saturday night. He had a negro man that shined shoes. I believe he had two chairs up front, you know, that sat up high, and the man would shine shoes and take care of the bathroom. When a man would get through getting his bath, then the

porter would go clean up the bathroom and get it ready for the next man who wanted to take a bath. Very few people had bathrooms in their houses. We called them bathrooms, but they didn't have—well, we all had outhouses and not many people had running water.

I remember that we had an underground cistern. The house right across the street was owned by one of the most influential men in the town, and he had an underground cistern. I remember that he had a kind of bucket thing, and he drew that up and then would pour water out into a little container that would run off into another bucket.

The man who lived on the corner was the cotton buyer. He also had a grocery store, but he was the cotton buyer. I remember that there was a particular phone that calls would come in on, and there was a little dog that they had up there, and if that phone rang, he would run to Mr. Scroggins and bark and Mr. Scroggins knew to go answer the phone and find out about the price of cotton. I grew up right here, and the Walkers were just about two blocks from my house.

Joe Zajicek also remembers the Walker family. At ninety-one years of age, he has lived in Buckholts, Texas, almost all of his life. Buckholts is eight miles from Rogers. Whitey Walker wasn't always at odds with the law, but like so many other restless young men of the small cotton towns in the 1920s, he had the need for "something to do."

Joe still operates heavy machine equipment to move dirt or level roadways. As Joe looked over some old photographs, he paused in concentration and tapped his finger on a mug shot in the photo book.

That's Whitey Walker. I've seen him many a time. He and his brother Hugh. Yeah, Hugh liked flipping coins when he was smoking cigars. That was a gambling game. He would wet one side of a coin from the spit of that cigar, that way when he tossed the coin, it would always land on the side he wanted. If anyone got wise to it, he would wipe it off and have those coins start hitting the other side. Hugh was a real good gambler. They would meet in different places to gamble. We used to have a little barbecue about every two weeks back in those days, and this bunch would show up once in a great while.

I think the bank here got robbed twice. Walker and Blackie Thompson were in on one robbery. Some of the locals thought it was a conspiracy. The hog business had free reign, and those people controlled the whole bottom. The people who owned the land couldn't farm it because these people had the land run over with the hogs and cattle.

Some fellas had some hog traps and wanted to start it big. They got a bunch of hogs, but they got that hog cholera and died. They just kicked those hogs in a slough and let them float off.

Yeah, they lost big money, and so they didn't want to lose what money was tied up with the bank. I can't prove it, but after the bank robbery you didn't hear nothing about anybody owing anything, because the bank was closed.

The Texas Panhandle in 1927 was a wild and dangerous place to live, and the oil boom towns in Borger, Stinnett, and especially a criminal hangout called Signal Hill were the worst. It was at Signal Hill that Whitey Walker, Blackie Thompson, Matt Kimes, Ace Pendleton, and a host of other outlaws stayed. It was there, a few miles from Stinnett in the middle of an oil-field, that robbers and cutthroats made plans, secured graft pay-offs to police and city officials, protected each other from nosey outsiders, and murdered on occasion.

In its early life, the town of Borger would feel martial law imposed by the governor, the use of Texas Rangers led by Frank Hamer (known for his role in the fatal ambush of Clyde Barrow and Bonnie Parker years later), and the infamous unsolved assassination of the district attorney Johnny Holmes. On March 31, 1927, in the nearby town of Pampa, the First National Bank was robbed by a group of men. Due to a series of events that included the murder of some public officials and prisoner escapes, no one was ever brought to trial for the bank robbery and the identities of the thieves remain officially unknown. One of the men identified was a member of both the Kimes and Cotton Top gangs, Whitey Walker.

Whitey had been on the run ever since a jail escape. In late March, 1927, two toughs named Clayton and Frazier Tontz were ordered arrested for a variety of crimes and were in the nearby Stinnett jail. The two brothers and Whitey Walker overpowered a jailer and escaped into Oklahoma. Frazier was killed while trying to escape from Sheriff John Russell of Okmulgee, Oklahoma.[1]

Eloise Lane is a writer in the town of Pampa, Texas, and in a partial reprint of her article published in the summer 1989 edition of *Focus* magazine, she tells the story of the robbery and its aftermath. Some of the original article has been changed with the author's permission due to information discovered after publication.[2]

One of the most exciting events ever to occur in the history of Pampa took place on Thursday, March 31, 1927. About 12:30 P.M., Blackie Thompson parked a seven-passenger Buick sedan parallel to the curb at the corner of Foster and Cuyler Streets. Matthew Kimes and "Whitey" Walker entered the bank through the south door where Owen Edwards remained as a guard. Ace Pendleton entered the bank sometime later.

One of the robbers, carrying a sack, walked up to cashier DeLea Vicars and teller A. V. Hendrick and told them to "Fill it up, make it quick, and nobody'll get hurt."

Several persons were in the bank when the robbers walked in, and these persons were quickly herded to the rear near the vault. As other people came into the bank, they were also shown the way to the vault. Some students who had come to the bank during their lunch hour were among them.

Joe Kahl, who was to be elected the most popular boy in the Pampa High School senior class of 1931, said that one robber "stuck a gun in me and told me to back up to the wall—and back up I did."

When Hazel Campbell (Mrs. Ray Wilson) unsuspectingly entered the bank, a robber pointed a gun at her and ordered: "Lady, step back into that vault."

One man, who was entering the vault, thought that the hold-up was a joke. He turned around and yelled, "Boo!" to the man who was holding a gun.

"Boo, hell!" snapped the robber as he brandished his gun. "Get back in that vault."

While the robbery was going on—it lasted ten to twenty minutes—J. E. Murfee Jr., Pampa dry goods merchant, came in with about $600 in silver and $500 in checks, which he intended to deposit. Just as Kimes started to take the money, he asked Murfee if the money was insured. Upon being told that the money was not insured, Kimes told Murfee to go ahead and make his deposit. Apparently, the robbers intended for the insurance company, rather than the bank's customers, to stand the loss of the robbery.

At one point during the robbery, one of the robbers made a trip outside to see about the large Buick sedan in which the bandits had come to the bank. By the time the robbers were ready to leave the bank, there were about thirty persons held at gunpoint near the vault. The robbers were about to lock all of them into the vault, when someone told the gunmen that a screwdriver would be needed to get out. Hesitating only a moment, the gunman quickly complied with the request when Mrs. L. C. McMurtry said in a formidable voice, "Give us that screwdriver!"

About that time, Edwards, who had been guarding the door, rushed to the others and shouted, "They're ganging up on the outside." Then the robbers turned the bars on the vault door, dashed outside to their waiting sedan, and sped away. It was later learned that the "gang outside" consisted of one man who was walking down the street with a gun over his shoulder, completely unaware of what had been going on inside the bank.

Several men, including Alvin B. Turner, were sitting on benches under the big locust trees in front of the White Deer Land Building. These men were employed to carry bricks to "Indian Jim" Brown, who was paving some of the streets of Pampa. As these men sat and ate their lunches, they had no idea of the excitement that was soon to permeate the city of Pampa.

The people inside the vault freed themselves in about three minutes because the vault had not been locked—only the bars were turned.

Other than those already named, the people in the vault included L. B. Haggard, Morris Seliger, C. H. Shoop, William Hulsey, W. W. Harrah, Troy Maness, Bruce Cobb, Flora Deen Finley, Frank Hopkins, Earl McFall, Roy McFall, Bill Jensen, Evan Shull, Ray Sellars, Rob Watson, A. E. Pfeiffer, and Ernest Fox.

Members of the bank staff in the vault were Helen Baird, Annette Hussey, A. V. Hendrick, and DeLea Vicars. Lorene Blanton was in an adjoining office and knew nothing about the robbery until those in the vault were freed. Bank cashier Edwin S. Vicars, who often complained that he missed everything exciting, had gone to lunch and missed this memorable event also.

Rufe Jordan, then a fourteen-year-old student at Kingsmill, had been sent on horseback to Pampa for seven rolls of crepe paper. He arrived at Pampa just after the robbery and was so interested in learning all the details that he was several hours late in returning to the school and was punished accordingly.

After the robbery, the bandits headed west and stopped at the home of W. E. Archer and his sister Robbie. The Archer home, on the road to Borger, was nearly two miles east of present Price Road. Some buildings behind the house were used for storing farm machinery and grain. The bandits parked their getaway car in the breezeway between buildings and entered the house a few at a time. The first men to enter asked to use the telephone because of "tire trouble." Just before the robbers reached the telephone, they drew guns and ordered the Archers to sit in chairs. The robbers asked if there were any firearms in the house and told the Archers that they would not be harmed if they acted normally. One of the bandits seemed nervous and "jumpy," but the others remained calm and made themselves "at home."

The invaders told the Archers about the robbery and looked at the loot, which included several diamond rings. They were especially pleased with a ring and a watch charm containing a ten-dollar gold piece belonging to the directors of the bank. The robbers expressed regret at having to inconvenience their host and hostess, and after the money was counted, all of them—robbers and residents—played cards.

Suddenly, as they sat in the living room, the telephone rang. At first it was decided to let the telephone ring unanswered, but since it was customary for Helen Baird's mother, a sister of the Archers, to call every day, the robbers decided that Robbie should take down the receiver.

As one of the bandits stood beside her, Robbie listened to her sister's account of the robbery, but she did not dare reveal that she already knew about the event and that the robbers were in her house. The sister was annoyed at Robbie because of her seeming indifference.

About 3:00 A.M. on Friday, April 1, the robbers prepared to leave. In a hall of the house there was a bathroom with a small window in the west. The bandits fastened the Archers inside this room by wedging a heavy two-by-four against the door. They told the Archers that when they reached Amarillo, they would telephone Pampa police to tell them of the plight of the prisoners.

Enos Archer, using a single-blade knife, cut out the panel of the door in about an hour and a half. He went immediately to Pampa to inform authorities about his uninvited guests.

Meanwhile, at Pampa, a final check of the bank's loss, approved by a bank examiner, showed $32,542 missing. Bills ranging from $1 to $100 in denomination and $1,700 in coins were taken. The bank had received a shipment of $15,000 on Wednesday, the day before the robbery. The bank expected to be paid its loss by the insurance company within a week.

Not long after the bank robbers fled the Archer home, stealing turned to murder. A well driller named Henry Fields reported to the Borger sheriff Joe Ownbey that he'd seen two dead men lying beside the Whittenburg Road, a mile out of town. There was an abandoned car nearby.[3] About fifteen minutes after the bandits left the Archers' house, two veteran deputies, Pat Kenyon and A. L. "Chick" Terry, were shot and killed on the road between Skellytown and Borger. The bodies of the deputies were found on the road, and their car was standing crosswise in the middle of the road. Apparently, the slain officers had been shot when they stopped their car to halt an approaching vehicle.[4] Kenyon had been shot in the head. Terry was shot through the right eye.[5]

Two loaded guns lay on the ground between them. Checking the guns, Sheriff Ownbey said, "There's been some switching of guns here. I gave Terry my white-handled pistol yesterday, but it ain't here now."[6] District attorney Douglas found some currency wrappings nearby. Mrs. Percy May lived not far from the tragedy and told officials that around 3:15 A.M. she had awakened to the sounds of gunshots with a car driving away afterward.[7]

The authorities went to Hugh Walker's house in Borger to ask him what he knew about the Pampa robbery. Hugh said he didn't know who robbed the bank. The sheriff and Rangers pressed him about his brother Whitey, and also regarding the whereabouts of Ed Bailey. Hugh asked them why they didn't ask Whitey himself. After all, the two were asleep in the back bedroom of the drugstore.

The two men denied any involvement in the robbery after being awakened. When Whitey began to put his socks on as he sat on the bed, the sheriff told him to get off the bed. When the lawman turned over the mattress, he uncovered the pearl-handled pistol that the sheriff had given one of the dead deputies. All three men were arrested, placed under $50,000 bond each, and taken to the Stinnett jail.[8] It was not for the two officers' deaths on the road that the trio was arrested, however. Whitey, Hugh, and Bailey were thrown in jail that morning for the March 19 shooting of a policeman named Coke Buchanan. The Dixon Creek officer died after being shot six times in a gunfight with five men. He had gone to the aid of Sam Williams, who was being beaten with pistols and was also a policeman.[9]

Once the word got out that the Walkers and Bailey were in jail, forty to fifty carloads of angry men headed toward Stinnett with the idea of a lynching. Three lawmen got the suspects out of jail and hid them under guard in a secluded canyon area miles from town. A posse was divided into groups and a sweep was made through the oil field and breaks looking for Matt Kimes and the rest of the gang.[10]

Eloise Lane continues:

> On Sunday, April 3, deputies and Texas Rangers raided a shack at Signal Hill. The story was told that a carload of Rangers came from Borger to arrest the outlaws, and as they came into Signal Hill, they encountered the outlaws in another car headed out of town at a high rate of speed. Evidently word had reached the robbers through the "underground" that the Rangers were on the way to arrest them. By the time the lawmen turned their car around, the bandits were gone, as if a hole had opened and swallowed them. In the exchange of gunfire when the cars crossed each other in and out of Signal Hill, no one was hurt. One car, abandoned near Electric City, contained several currency wrappers for the loot taken from the Pampa bank.[11]

While half of the Panhandle police and sheriff's departments were looking for Kimes, Terrell and Ace Pendleton (who

were later considered innocent of the Pampa robbery), Texas
Ranger Frank Hamer was furious that the local police in Borger
were tipping off the outlaws so that they could keep getting away
from any capture by Hamer's men.[12]

Meanwhile, back in Stinnett, the Walkers had made bond
and skipped town. One report says that Bailey, unable to make
bond, agreed to testify against the brothers if they were caught
again.[13] Another report states that all three were released on
$7,500 bond each; Hugh on April 19; Bailey, April 28; and
Walker, May 14.[14] As soon as Whitey got out, all three skipped
town. Whitey knew things were too hot to stay around, but he
wanted to let everyone in town know how he felt about the situation. The day he skipped town, the outlaw sent a note to the
local newspaper, the *Borger Herald*. The note read, "I am leaving for awhile until I can get a fair trial. I don't want to be the
goat of a frame-up." It also showed the chivalrous side of
Whitey, or else showed a glimpse of his inner thoughts on the
issue of law and order versus the criminal element: "I have always played fair," claimed Walker. Pressure from the Texas
Rangers forced a mass resignation of the courthouse gang,
along with the chief of police and nearly all of the police force.[15]

Whether Whitey was arrested again or willingly appeared
for trial is unclear, but in December 1927 he made a sensation-
al escape from a Hutchinson County courtroom.[16] The disappearance of the gang had the newspapers dubbing them the
"Ghost Bandits." The white-handled pistol had come back to
haunt one of the Ghost Bandits, and he was being tried for the
slaying of deputy sheriff A. L. Terry.

Whitey and Pendleton, who were still wanted for the Pampa
bank robbery, teamed up to create mayhem across a seven-state
area. With the aid of various accomplices during their time on
the run, they robbed banks in Wyoming, New Mexico, Colorado, Oklahoma, Texas, Arkansas, and Louisiana. Their recruited gang members were some of the most dangerous people
in the Texas Panhandle—murderers and heavy hitters, each
and every one of them. One of their accomplices was Owen Edwards, an accused killer of police officers Terry and Kenyon
after the Pampa robbery. Another was Fred Nave, a dance hall
operator in Borger and murderer of a man named Jack Mor-

gan. Nave lived in Childress, Texas. The other gang member was Clayton Tontz, who was a murderer and highjacker. Clayton's charge with the killing of Amarillo druggist John Langley had been thrown out on a technicality, due to lack of evidence, so he may be the only exception to a murderer label.[17]

On September 19, 1928, Whitey, Clayton Tontz, and Edwards robbed the bank at Covington, Oklahoma, getting away with $20,000. There was a running gun battle with police; however, the bandits escaped. The next day Tontz's body was found near Stroud, Oklahoma, with a bullet in the heart. About six weeks later, Owen Edwards was killed in a gunfight with officers at Harjo, Oklahoma, a town about twenty-five miles from Seminole, following a bank robbery. Police Officer Jim Kiersey died in that shootout.

On January 15, 1929, Whitey and Fred Nave were arrested in Buffalo, New York, by Detective Sgt. McCarty, who recognized both of them from photos on wanted posters. The two men were well-dressed and wore expensive jewelry. McCarty told Hutchinson County Sheriff Joe Ownbey that "their whiskers, which they had grown for a disguise, attracted my attention."

Whitey and Nave had given fictitious names and claimed that they had arrived in Buffalo in their private airplane and were leaving for Florida shortly. Whitey told McCarty that his name was Clyde Roberts, but he was arrested under the name Walter Anderson.[18] McCarty took the two men to police headquarters, fingerprinted both, and put their photos on the wire. Captain Frank Hamer telegraphed McCarty that both men were escape artists and to watch them closely. He did. A policeman armed with a tear gas bomb and sawed-off shotgun sat in front of their cells. Another, similarly armed, was stationed outside the locked door of the cell room, while a third stood guard on the ground floor of the police station.[19]

Harper and Sheriff Fred Bowles of Ada, Oklahoma, traveled to Buffalo to pick up the two outlaws for a Lamar, Colorado, bank robbery and the murder of four men at the bank. Whitey was wanted for murder, but Nave at that time was wanted only for liquor violations and for jumping $500 bond in Pampa. Twelve detectives helped Chief Harper and Sheriff Bowles put the two on the train for Colorado.

It was found later that George J. Anshier, Howard L. Roys-
ton, and Ralph Fleagle robbed the Lamar bank and killed the
four men. When Harper learned of his mistake, the two outlaws
were released to Texas authorities to stand trial. Colorado
Governor W. H. Adams ordered Walker and Nave turned over
to Texas officials following a two-day extradition hearing. Oklahoma officers wanted Walker for bank robbery[20] at Nardin,
Oklahoma, and several other states wanted him, but Texas got
him.

Clem Calhoun, appointed district attorney following
Johnny Holmes' assassination, wrote Governor Moody that "we
do not have any case at all against Whitey Walker that we can
expect to get a conviction in. Sheriff Fred Bowles of Ada,
Oklahoma, is here now for Walker. From all the information I
can gather they have the best case against him."

Walker was in the Stinnett jail from October 1, 1929, to
November 4, 1929. That was the day he tried to escape.
Believing that he was being taken to another county for safe-
keeping from some rather irate Hutchinson County citizens,
Whitey told his brother Hugh that he "was going to Dallas, I
expect."[21]

Texas Ranger W. H. Kirby and Sheriff C. O. Moore took
Whitey about two miles toward Borger, where, to Walker's surprise, Oklahoma officers were waiting for him. When he was told
he was going to Oklahoma, Whitey yelled, "I'll be damned if I
do," and tried to leap out of the car. He didn't make it. He was
transferred to a second car with Sheriff Bowles and one of his
deputies inside.[22] Both officers carried rifles and machine guns.

It's understandable that Walker didn't want to return to
Oklahoma. There were too many charges against him there. He
had robbed the banks at Purcell, Newkirk, Lamont, Nardin,
Prague, and the First National at Allen, to name a few.[23]
Following trial in Oklahoma, he was sentenced to the penitentiary at McAlester for ninety-nine years on December 12, 1929,
as prisoner #21283 for robbery with firearms.[24]

Meanwhile, the charge of murder against Hugh Walker for
the killing of Coke Buchanan was dismissed for "lack of evidence." Hugh moved to Lubbock, where he opened a gambling
hall. He shot Frank V. Brown because Brown refused to return

$1,000 he had won in Hugh's place. Walker was sent to Huntsville for ninety-nine years but was released within three years.[25]

After a series of escapes and con man tricks to fool police in several different encounters, Ace Pendleton was arrested in Odessa, Texas, on December 8, 1930. When he was sent to Pampa, he became ill before the trial and was moved from the jail to the jury room by order of county physician V. E. von Brunow.[26] He was attended by a special nurse and two deputies at different times. Strangely, the young man who was scolded for not returning to school in time after the Pampa robbery, Rufe Jordan, sometimes sat with his dad, Frank, who was the daytime deputy watching Pendleton. Pendleton must have liked the high school senior, because he gave him his shaving razor.[27] Ace could buy another one because he had won again. His ailments had all but broken the county budget at fifteen dollars a day in expenses. It had become a financial nightmare to keep him locked up to heal.

On April 5, 1933, District Attorney Lewis Goodrich petitioned the judge of the 31st Judicial Court of Gray County, Texas, to dismiss criminal action No. 336, State of Texas v. Ace Pendleton. The reason was that "the evidence available is insufficient to warrant a conviction."

As for Rufe Jordan, he would use that razor he was given for the next sixty-two years, many of those years as a lawman in his own right.[28]

Whitey Walker would have his chance again later. This spree, enough for a lifetime for most bandits, was just the beginning for the man from Rogers, Texas. It was time to meet, or find again, Irvin "Blackie" Thompson. Whitey would also meet Roy Johnson. It was time to try somehow to get back to Texas, to get back home. Whitey Walker had a plan, and he needed it to get out of this mess.

CHAPTER 2

The Rest of the Crew

Roy Alvin Johnson, the youngest of what was to become the Whitey Walker Gang, had been in trouble since he was fifteen years old, and he had been out in the real world since he was only eleven. He was born October 2, 1904, in Brownwood, Texas, to Viola and Frank Sexton, but his father was killed in an accident in 1907. In 1909 Viola married Wallace Johnson, and Roy went by that last name when he wasn't using an alias. One of four children, Roy left the family before his mother separated from Wallace in 1920. She later married a man named Jack Farmer, and the family moved to Oklahoma City.

Roy lived his childhood in Oklahoma, and he managed to complete the fifth grade at a rural school there in 1916. When he was eleven, right after the fifth grade, he tried to join the army but was obviously not allowed to because of his age. After that he drifted to the wheat fields of Kansas for a couple of years, working as he could until he could get something steady. For eight months in 1917, he worked as a water boy at Pickening, Arkansas, for Pratt Engineering Company. Then Roy went to Shelbyville, Tennessee, where he worked until November 11, 1919.[1]

In Dodge City, Kansas, he had his first real brush with the law, using the alias Roy Sexton in a stickup on July 11, 1922. Either the charges were dropped, or else he served a light sen-

17

tence, because Johnson was working for two years operating electrical motors for the Dupont Engineering Company near the same time period. When the young man left Dupont, he did odd jobs in the oil fields, traveling over Kansas, Oklahoma, and Texas until 1923. In that year he was hired by the Missouri Pacific Railroad as a fireman and worked about six months, until the rushing season was finished. Then it was again time to move down the road.[2]

It was in 1925 that Roy got his chance as a ball player, and he played throughout the Midwest. Life was looking up for Roy, but he couldn't handle his booze very well. Prohibition was in full swing, and Roy got in a jam when he was drunk in Medford, Oklahoma. Life for Roy would change dramatically on June 28, 1925, with the orange flare of one bullet shot in a moment of panic. Roy was no longer a ball player, but was now a murderer implicated in a botched burglary with a couple of buddies. By Roy's own admission, he and two others (prison records show that Roy would tell what happened in any situation if apprehended), one of whom was Albert Greer and the other of whom was never caught, were in a car in Medford. The three men were planning a burglary, when a deputy sheriff came up to them and started shooting. Roy and his partners started shooting back, and the deputy sheriff was killed. Whoever actually fired didn't matter, because Roy was too drunk to run before he was arrested.[3]

The ex–ball player was sentenced to be electrocuted in Oklahoma on May 22, 1926, but that sentence was commuted to life on October 16, 1926, by the Court of Criminal Appeals.[4] Instead, he was sent to serve his life sentence at the Oklahoma State Prison in McAlester on January 27, 1926. Not ready to spend the rest of his life in an Oklahoma prison, Roy escaped in January 1932. Supposedly his mother secured a recommendation from all members of the jury for Roy's release, which in turn had been given to the governor, then to the pardoning attorney.

Whatever actually happened at this point is speculation, because during the late 1920s and early 1930s graft was the name of the game. It is well documented that during the Ma and Pa Ferguson years, pardons, furloughs, and general graft agreements were bought and sold like cattle on the hoof. According to Roy Johnson's explanation of the story, his mother approached the pardoning attorney, and the attorney stated that he did not have any papers to release Roy, after she had been told that everything was set; instead he asked her if she had any money. When Viola told her son this, he knew that he had no way of getting out except by getting some money. So he escaped.[5]

He had been in charge of the photography department and was a trustee when he bolted from the prison. Johnson didn't stay on the run for very long. In less than a month, the escaped convict was looking for money to buy a pardon, when he was arrested in Oscala, Florida, on February 5, 1932, for breaking and entering. Roy was returned to the Oklahoma Penitentiary on February 16 with no money, no pardon, and no hope of being anywhere but prison. Bad company and too much whiskey had finished chances of a decent life early for the young man.[6] He didn't know at the time that Whitey Walker and Irvin "Blackie" Thompson were on their way to the same prison, and they were determined *not* to stay in any prison for long. Roy would soon be on a long ride with some heavy hitters.

IRVIN *"BLACKIE"* THOMPSON

Irvin Thompson was born May 9, 1893, to a family that lived in Wheeler County, Texas, but he may have been born in either Arkansas or Oklahoma. His family were railroad people, migrating as the railroad lines progressed.[7] His name was Irvin Thompson, but his family called him "Blackie" if he made them mad.[8] Everybody else apparently called him Blackie because the quarter-Cherokee had jet-black hair and a dark complexion. His parents were Georgia and William Thompson, with brothers Frank and Morris, sisters Ethel May and Pearl.[9] Thompson was a shoemaker by trade, possibly from prison instruction.

According to legendary Texas Ranger Clint Peoples, Thompson was "The meanest man I ever handled in Montgomery County."[10] Thompson even used the Ranger's last name as an alias during an arrest in Florida. (He used the last name Peoples; whether it was for the Texas Ranger or not was an assumption made by the ranger.)[11] One thing was for certain: Blackie was not a man to be taken for granted or tangled with lightly.

His family said he never talked about his business in the house, never brought any outlaws with him on visits, and never raised his voice, assuming he said anything at all.[12] W. J. Ford was a nephew of Blackie Thompson and played many a domino game with him as a sixteen-year-old boy. There are things that W. J. will talk about regarding his uncle, but for the most part the specifics of Blackie Thompson's life will never be told.[13]

Thompson's first term in the penitentiary came on November 21, 1920, when he became prisoner #10916 at McAlester, Oklahoma, where he had been sentenced to five years for larceny of an automobile.[14]

This was less than a year after he had attended the funeral for his grandmother in Oklahoma.[15] He was paroled on March 6, 1922. After fifteen months on parole, he robbed a bank in Chickasaw, Oklahoma. It didn't take long after that robbery for his arrest in Joplin, Missouri, on December 22, 1923, and he was returned to Oklahoma. Whitey Walker was also implicated in the robbery, and it was clear that these men were partners in crime as early as 1923, despite claims that they didn't meet until a prison stint in 1933. Thompson's parole was revoked on May 14, 1924.[16]

He evidently escaped, because he was picked up in May of 1924 for robbery and received a twenty-five-year sentence. Thompson promptly escaped again but was arrested on December 24, 1934, at Bartlesville, Oklahoma, for murder. He had killed a deputy sheriff in Creek County. It was rumored that he killed the deputy because he was harassing Thompson for being an Indian. What a case of baiting the bear![17] So, Blackie had a new entry for February 9, 1925, when he was received at McAlester with a life sentence for murder. At McAlester he was now tagged with two terms, one for twenty-five years and one for life.[18] There he remained until June 17, 1926, when he was transferred to the state reformatory at Granite, Oklahoma. He was returned to McAlester. The opportunity for the escape did not come until the summer of 1933.[19] His wife, Virginia, would just have to wait in the wings. It was time for the Fishing-Hole Gang to come together.

CHAPTER 3

Rogers Bound,
Buckholts Will Do

On August 30, 1933, two convicted murderers and a bank robber, all serving life terms in the Oklahoma State Penitentiary, escaped from the prison farm at McAlester. Whitey Walker, Blackie Thompson, and Roy Johnson asked a guard for permission to go fishing at the prison farm lake. They didn't go fishing for long, and they didn't come back. The trio managed to get a ride out of Oklahoma to begin a six-month crime spree throughout the Texas Panhandle and Central and East Texas.

It is not clear where the gang went during September, but according to Captain Clint Peoples, the trio went to the oil fields near Conroe, where they could move about with ease due to the high number of people in the oil boom area. This transient environment is what worked so well at Borger and Signal Hill.[1] Ranger Peoples claimed that Blackie Thompson shot and killed a taxi cab driver after an argument and was captured by the Texas Ranger while Thompson was eating in a local cafe. Thompson had a concealed .45 automatic pistol, but Ranger Peoples arrested him without incident.[2] The Ranger further stated that Walker and Johnson were already in the Montgomery County jail when he placed Thompson there, and the three smashed the old cement floor and dug a tunnel with their hands, eventually tunneling under the jailhouse foundation. Aided by a

21

fourth man, they escaped, but all were recaptured by the next morning. Despite the escape attempt, Thompson, Walker, and Johnson were able to make bond and disappear again.[3]

Whatever happened to them in September, there was no doubt about their whereabouts by the first week of October 1933. Whitey Walker had plenty of friends in his hometown of Rogers, and while the Panhandle was being searched for the escapees' trail, Walker went home.

The community of Rogers was eight miles from another community, called Buckholts. Like scores of other hamlets in Texas, Buckholts was a small farming area during the Great Depression.

Joe Zajicek has lived in Buckholts or Rogers nearly all his life and tells a brief history:

> I think it was my uncle, my mother's brother, they had two little gins, but it took thirty minutes to gin a bale of cotton. They had one, and then they got another one so that they could gin two bales an hour that way. Now to gin a bale, I think it's less than ten minutes to bale. They would haul cotton in one-bale wagons.
>
> Well, I recollect the teens and it wasn't too bad. Then, by 1925 it got pretty bad, but when it come into the '30s, it started hitting us *real* bad. That's when people began moving into town from the country.
>
> They just went and did what they could for work. My mother had two brothers, those that had those gins, they had farms too. Grandpa had at one time better than a section of land. He divided it all. They sold the land and moved to Little River, and that's when that sandstorm hit them. In the '20s and '21. Down here, we had floods. So they left it. They went off and left it, and the people that stayed there bought the land for taxes later on. Those people got rich. Some of the people who had left said, "Yeah, you're the one got our land. Now y'all got rich." Their answer was, "Well, we weren't rich enough to leave and had to stay, so it's compensation."

On October 6, 1933, the Whitey Walker Gang would start the first of a string of robberies and kidnappings. In Buckholts, just miles from Walker's parents' home, the bank was open for business. In an article in the *Temple Daily Telegram* on October 7, 1933, one of the few coherent coverages of the robbery is discussed in detail.

One must be aware, however, that newspapers are not completely reliable sources. In researching the Whitey Walker Gang, many reports have proven to be speculation, rumor, innuendo, and heat-of-the-moment misinformation written as fact. To compound that problem, news coverage during this time period was often a reporter from a nearby area writing a story in the morning to be distributed by the Associated Press for the evening papers regionally. If parts of a story were wrong to begin with, that misinformation was copied by many other papers that were using the identical article. The point is that just because an event is cited in fifteen different newspapers, the reality is that it is the same potentially flawed coverage. This is even more of a problem when the coverage, flawed or not, contradicts witnesses. When a small-town bank is robbed, people may not be thinking clearly in the aftermath. This particular article, from the *Telegram,* is a good example of all of these elements:

> Three men, who brazenly halted their car by the roadside just outside of Buckholts to divide the money, robbed the Buckholts State Bank of $3,000 at 9:30 A.M. yesterday. Last night officers had found no trace of the men.
>
> A third man seated in a Plymouth coupe outside the bank sped away with the two men after the robbery and police have been unable to get trace of them since the robbery.
>
> Ed Kolba, president of the bank, and Leo Fuchs, cashier, were at the bank when two middle aged men, dressed in new striped overalls, one wearing a grey cap and the other a slouch hat, and four day beards, entered the front door. The two men separated at the door without slowing their pace. One stepped to the window at the front of the bank and the other proceeded along the row of windows toward the back door where he pointed a pistol at Mr. Kolba and ordered him into the front of the bank. Mr. Fuchs received a similar order.
>
> When the robber put the pistol against Mr. Kolba's back and ordered him to the front of the building, Mr. Kolba tried to attract the attention of T. V. Adams, attorney whose offices are in the rear of the bank, but Mr. Adams, unaware that the

robbers were in the bank, never raised his head from his books. It was not until he turned to a typewriter and began writing that the robbers saw him. He too, was ordered on to the floor of the front office.

Mr. Kolba told the robbers that there was no need to rough them, that there was nothing in the bank which could be used to harm them. The men heeded their request and told them to act quickly and they would not be bothered.

He said the men looked nervous when they walked into the bank and that the man who leaned over the counter at the back of the bank to point the pistol at him continued to look that way. But when he put the revolver to his back, Mr. Kolba said, the robbers hand never shook and the gun felt "as steady as a rod."

Mr. Fuchs was greeted with the words: "You're the man we want. Get down on the floor." The man grabbed his arm and commanded him again to act quickly.

Both men agreed that the robbers looked like hardened criminals. Mr. Kolba stated that he could identify the men that accosted him.

W. H. Walker [not Whitey Walker], bank customer, walked into the bank to cash two checks and was ordered inside the cage and to lie down before he realized that he had walked in on a robbery.

Walker's entrance into the bank caused no alarm to the robbers. They saw him before he knew that he was walking in on a bank robbery. They told him "come on big boy, you can come back here and lie down too." He was surprised and said, "pardon me," but he came to the spot pointed out.

In a hurried rifling of the cash drawers and vault the men overlooked $2,000 in currency and a large amount of silver coins. When through with their work, one of them said "Let's go." His companion said, "Let's lock them in the vault," and the other answered that maybe they "had better take one of them with us."

They decided not to take a prisoner with them and ordered the men into the vault. Mr. Kolba explained that they would be suffocated if the door of the vault was locked and the men agreed only to close the door.

They went out to their car, handed the money to the driver and started south by the bank from which they were parked and turned and went west on Highway 36. One man said he saw three men in a coupe dividing money by the side of the road just outside of Buckholts.

The car had been driven around the block and in front of the bank before the robbery. One man got out of the car about a block below the bank and walked to the bank. The other came with the driver, who waited outside. The two men entered the door at the same time, but had come to the bank from different directions. Both the men had .45 caliber revolvers, not automatic, Mr. Kolba said.

A witness standing across the street from the bank remarked that "they are sure putting a lot of money into that car." But he said later that it never occurred to him or his companions that the bank was being robbed.

Henry Ashcraft and V. H. Hopkins remarked that they saw the men but never suspected anything wrong. One man, Mr. Hopkins said, was about 5 feet 7 inches tall and weighed about 135 or 140 pounds. The other man, he said, was taller and huskier.

He said that the man came out of the front door of the bank and walked down the sidewalk by the bank as if going to Walschak gin, but suddenly cut to the left toward the Texas Farm Bureau gin. He then, without speeding his pace, walked to the car and got in.

Joe Zajicek was a witness to events as they occurred after the robbery, and he saw events a bit differently as he pursued the bank robbers:

I was twenty-five or twenty-six during the bank robbery.

I was working for the shop that's where the old bank was, on the corner down there where that phone office is now. I was working right across the street in that shop, yeah, it's a big double building, it's still there. I had a '31 Chevy and a double barrel shotgun in the back of it. There was a boy working in there, and he run out in the street and he said, "Bank robber, bank robber!"

The street went straight and then it turned towards the railroad track. It just curved through town, not straight like it is now. I looked up there and seen the back of a car making dust, and I jumped in that car of mine and I followed them through Rogers and into what they called Reed Lake Road, the other side of Rogers, 'cause those were gravel roads and I followed the dust, big dust, you know, you couldn't lose them.

When I got pretty close to their nesting place or whatever, I started thinking. I said they got them big guns and I got this shotgun—man, what the heck am I doing? At the time, by then, I had some time to think it over, and I saw me with a double barrel and them with automatics and everything.

Well, I seen the road that turned off the road and it was all wooded, see. There's thick woods there and after you got so far, you couldn't see in there. So, when I seen that dust turn in there, and I'd done thought about that, I just went on over to Val Verde and came on home and back to the shop and went to work.

Well, I jumped and run off, didn't tell nobody nothing. I just jumped in there and took off myself, come back and didn't say nothing no more because I figured they'd [the Whitey Walker Gang] be liable to look me up. I kept quiet. A number of farmers who gathered around the bank after the hold-up expressed the hope that their notes had been stolen too.

In the chaos and excitement of the robbery, everyone seemed to see the escaping bandits leaving town in all different directions. One thing was for sure—they had successfully escaped.

The Plymouth car in which the men escaped had been stolen from a Fort Worth postman. It had a long nickel-plated horn between the front lights, and it was dark blue or black with yellow wheels.[4]

Everett Mitchell, a small boy at the time, was at the junction of Highway 36 and Highway 2B south of Little River and said that he saw a coupe shortly after the robbery but did not know how many men were in the car nor what the license number was.

Sheriff Mobley of McLennan County passed through Belton and told Bell County Sheriff George Zivley that he was about fifteen minutes behind a Plymouth coupe headed toward Austin. The community of Sparks called authorities in Belton that a car answering the general description of the robbers' car had passed through at 9:30, but no one knew where the bandits went.[5] Another man telephoned Temple police, saying he had seen the car west of Rogers on its way to Temple. Temple police guarded the highway, but the car never came past Little River, six miles south of Temple. State Highway Patrolmen Boyd Wyatt and J. T.

Yarborough came to Temple from the highway near Little River, where they had been patrolling. The patrolmen changed from motorcycles to an automobile so that they could scout the county roads near the Leon and Lampasas river bottoms.[6]

Joe Zajicek thought more about what he had seen so many years ago. He remembered the Walker family before the string of bank robberies and kidnappings:

> We danced polka, waltzes. All of them at the dance hall down the road.
>
> Whitey used to break in that hall when we had checkers. People would go out there and check their big overcoats and hats and they'd check them while they were dancing. They would break into the room and steal a bunch of those checks and then come up there and try to claim the overcoat or hat or something like that. They stole them I guess a week or so before or right after the dance. Then they were in town the following week.
>
> I've seen Whitey more than once. He had one of them checks one time or two and he was in town on the street. My uncle, my father's brother, was the caretaker of the hall. He was trying to get him to pay $60 for an overcoat that he took over there. He was getting rough with [my] uncle, and he just had what they call the sheriff that used to go on a turning plow, the cutting blade. He had just had it sharpened at a blacksmith shop. He got it by the point and was holding it so Whitey knew it was time to back off.
>
> Yeah, he got the message. He kept on, he says, "You all didn't put nothing like that over here and I ain't given you a damn thing." He had that cigar in his mouth. He wouldn't back up until he saw that thing in his hand, and he got the message.

The bank was insured against theft, and the depositors and the bank were both protected. The exact amount taken from the bank was $2,903.[7] Chances of capturing the gang was increased when it was discovered that nine Confederate pension checks were included in the stolen money, and payment of the checks was stopped.[8]

The day I interviewed him, Zajicek looked out the window of his house. A large stock tank covered much of the acreage in his front yard. He said:

Oh, yeah, I remember when we were kids, we'd pull tricks on people. Just like model T days, people would change their coils and they'd have four coils and they'd ignite the spark plug, we'd change one in there backwards and they'd run on three cylinders and we'd change two of them and it'd sound like an old John Deere tractor. Times were a lot different back then . . .

CHAPTER 4

Hit at Palestine

Lester Hamilton leaned forward to look at the old photos of the gangsters who had been dead for sixty-five years. His wife, Frances, sat on a couch nearby. She was not from Palestine originally, but she had left Tennessee in time to see the railroads, the Great Depression, a World War, and civil strife in the East Texas town that was once considered the capital of East Texas. The railroads were the death of the majestic steamboats and the nearby town of Magnolia that thrived on the steamboats. The last steamboat run carried the very railroad supplies that would kill the river industry.

The old trolley that took eager townspeople from the courthouse to downtown and back was sold to the city of Dallas long, long, ago. The downtown today is a series of renovated buildings that house antique and curio shops. There are still local merchants that have somehow kept their head above the pounding waves of Wal-Mart and Target superstores. When a person walks down the street in Palestine, a stranger can ask directions or simply say hello without fear of being rebuffed as an outsider. There is a local newspaper called the *Palestine Daily Herald*. Lester Hamilton was editor of that paper through the Great Depression and many years afterward, and his father ran the show before him.

Lester shifted positions in his most comfortable chair.

Crippled with arthritis, he did the best he could to ease the pain. He put the photo collection on the footstool next to him and smiled for an instant as he remembered events long ago, so distant:

Many years ago, the railroad was in steam operation at Palestine. They had a general office and a shop with about 600 men working there. There was a strike; it was after the first war—about 1920, I'd say, there was a railroad strike that took in the whole railroad set-up. The railroad built a bullpen fence all the way around their property, which covered a lot of ground, and stationed a man with a shotgun about every fifty feet around that whole fence on the inside. On the outside of the fence were the striking workers. Things got so tense in the town that the governor, I suppose it was, sent the Rangers in here. I remember it well. These two Rangers—one took a downtown street, and the other took the next downtown street and they'd just walk around in the street; that settled any violence. Not a head was pumped or anything. Those two Rangers, all they had to do was expose themselves. That was an old-time Ranger.

Well, my mother wouldn't turn away anybody who wanted food, that's for sure. The police here picked up one of these men. They came in and literally hunted him to our house. One of them went and knocked on her door, the police picked him up for some reason—just talked to him, didn't arrest him, and took a note out of one of his pockets. The note had written: "708 South Sycamore, Palestine. Big dog, but friendly." We had a big collie dog at the time.

The reason Palestine got so many of those men during the depression was the East Texas Oil field was discovered right at that time, and there wasn't any way to move the oil, you know, overnight more or less. So, an oil train came through Palestine about every fifteen to twenty minutes. As close together as they could by law to being there. The two downtown main streets cross the railroad. If you wanted to go to town in Palestine, you were going to have to stand there while a freight train went by. Every time a train came through, these men would jump off of it—up to a hundred men would pour off these trains into Palestine. Of course some of them caught the next train out, but a lot of them stayed for some reason or another. The town was covered up with them more or less. They'd mark the curbs, and that would tell the others whether a house was good or bad. My mother got a good report! The men appreciated it. They weren't tramps; they were just men out of work and trying to find a place to live. She invited them in and seated them.

Anyway, one of these men went to our neighbors' door, I remember, and they fed him and he wanted to do something for them. He said, "What can I do?"

Well, they were leaving for some reason and told him nothing [needed] to be done. When they got home, their place had been landscaped beautifully. It was that kind of situation.

My family ran one paper, the *Palestine Herald Press.* It was the *Herald* at the time. There was a competitor paper, *The Palestine Press.* The *Press* was a morning paper, and, of course, our family paper was in the afternoon. The people at the press worked until one or two in the morning. They'd pile up discarded papers, old papers, always a lot of that kind of paper. They'd bundle it up, I say bundle it, they kept it for these men. They called them *Hoover blankets.* A pad of old newspapers will keep you pretty warm. The *Press* would give them a pad of old papers, and they'd go to bed with them. As for where these men slept, I believe they slept at an old foundry that was here or else on the ground.

Lester's wife, Frances, looked puzzled and turned to her husband, asking, "Was that the Dilly Foundry?"
He continued:

Yes, the foundry was in operation then. It covered a lot of ground. They had a big building that had been abandoned, where most of the men slept. Now, that didn't cover them all, and I don't know where the rest went.

My father, he'd give people a stack of papers for a nickel. I said why do you bother with that? A nickel doesn't buy you anything, why don't you just give them the paper. He said, "Well, if I charge them for it, they'll use them. There's not an unlimited supply; lots of the country people use them for wallpaper, you know. He said if we charge them a nickel, they're not going to come down here and bum the papers. If I see they really need them, I don't charge them the nickel."

Palestine wasn't always a downtown reminiscing its past; during the oil boom of the nearby fields, the cotton coming to the several gins, and the railroads transporting commerce through the heart of town, it was the hub of East Texas. One of the many downtown businesses was the Robinson Guaranty State Bank and Trust Company. The officers in 1928 were Z. L. Robinson, president; Guy T. Robinson, vice president; and William B. Robinson, cashier.

The Robinson Bank was located at 314 Main Street and took up the length of the building to Oak Street. It was a very solid operation. It was said that the officers of the bank could liquidate their assets and pay all depositors their accounts with just one day's notice. It is also proof of the bank's soundness that it was the first bank in Texas that was notified to reopen after President Franklin Roosevelt ordered banks closed during the early days of his administration.[1]

On October 26, 1933, twenty days after the Buckholts bank robbery, four people waited outside the Robinson State Bank and Trust Company. The Whitey Walker Gang was ready for more action, this time at Palestine's expense. Enoch Henry, the porter, came to the bank at 7:30 A.M. Two men crowded in the front door immediately behind him and pulled revolvers, while two stayed outside in the car. Both men who entered the bank were dressed in plain clothes and wearing hats. One of them was of a stocky build, and the other was wearing a pair of dark glasses.[2]

The two robbers forced Henry to go about his routine chores, ordering him to leave the door unlocked and raise the shades as usual. Enoch, who was a preacher as well as the bank porter, was hog-tied and forced to lie on the floor.[3] They gagged him and then tied his thumbs together with wire. He was bound by the teller cages. Enoch told people years later that the robbers had leather belts that they put around the bank employee's necks and then nailed the belts to the floor. The floor of the bank was wooden, so the employees were trapped on the floor to keep them out of the way while the outlaws went about their business.[4] The unmasked bandits methodically waylaid bank officials one by one as they entered the building.

C. O. Miller Jr., assistant cashier, was the second to arrive, at 7:40 A.M. The two robbers stepped out from behind a desk and pointed their pistols at the cashier. He was forced to open the vault and get out some silver, then to lie on the floor. "I had to work the combination twice before I could open it," Miller declared. "They put something around my neck while I was working on it but removed it when I finished. They were careful not to let us look at them very closely. One of them was very nervous, but the other one acted like an old-timer at the business." (This was a recurring theme with these robberies, and it appears that Walker was calm while Thompson was anxious to get the job done and leave). Miller was also forced to open a money till in the main safety vault.

Will and Lee Robinson were next to arrive, and it was the same routine, lie on the floor. The bandits forced Will Robinson to open the safe by threatening Lee Robinson's life. Unfortunately for the gang, the time lock was set for 10:00 A.M. that morning, so all they got were the contents of the minor safe, not the big vault.[5] One of the gunmen threatened to kill the cashier when it was learned that the time lock on the safety vault would not be off for two hours.[6] The safe was located near the front of the bank, near the president's office. The thieves seized all the loose currency in the small safe, together with an undetermined number of checks. Bank president Z. L. Robinson entered and was likewise waylaid and forced to lie on the floor.

The outlaws scooped up silver and currency amounting to around $5,500.[7] After looting the safe, the bandits then forced the bank officials into the main vault in the rear of the building. The officials were locked in the vault. Once inside, the captives triggered a tear gas device, causing the bandits to leave.

From every indication, the bank robbery had been well mapped.

" 'We hate like hell to do this, but it has to be done,' " Mr. Robinson quoted one of the gunmen as saying. According to witnesses, Enoch said, "I was just praying as hard as I could, and Mr. Charles was over there just a-cussing!"

"Mr. Robinson was a person that was very definite. He was an outdoor person, a sportsman, and I have an idea that he didn't take anything off those guys and that may have been the reason that they didn't use some of the techniques that they had done before," Mrs. Surles, a friend of Mr. Robinson, related.

The gunmen ran out with the money in a white sack, tossed

it onto the fender of the waiting car, and drove slowly away with two other men who waited in the Ford V-8 sedan (one of the "men" could have been Mrs. Dolly Walker).

District Clerk Jim M. Moore said he was sitting in his car directly across from the bank when the robbery occurred. "The money sack remained on the fender when the car drove off," Moore said. "The stocky-built man got in the front seat with the waiting driver.

"They came out right after the tear gas exploded," he related. "In the car in front were two men, one sitting at the wheel and the other on the back seat." Moore realized that a robbery had occurred and later identified the car for the police. Officers obtained the number of the car and left in pursuit.

"There was parallel parking at that time, you see. They could get right up to it. We didn't have the one-way streets. That came in the '40s. We had so many of the army groups that were coming from Temple through to Louisiana that they would have to block off the streets, and that was when they made these one-way streets," Mrs. Surles explained.

Moore followed the car around the depot, where it turned east on Spring Street. The bandits drove on eastward past the Home Ice Company and turned onto Highway 19 at the Independent Lumber Company. This gesture, the district clerk believed, was only a ruse, as officers later learned the men had turned back and headed west on Highway 43. The entire loss was covered by insurance. "We had every kind of insurance we could get," Mr. Robinson stated. Z. L. Robinson, president of the bank, said the total amount of the loot was approximately $5,500, including $3,100 in currency, $1,200 in silver, $200 in government coupon bonds, and $1,000 in unsigned registered bonds.[8]

Several people who heard the teargas explosion saw the car drive away. The highway license number given was 385-373. Sheriff's officers learned positively that the highway license plates on the robbers' car were the same plates stolen from an automobile belonging to Monroe Anderson, near Marlin in Falls County, two weeks before. Deputy Sheriff John England said the numbers had been checked by the tax collector of Falls County and by the Falls County Sheriff.

Jim Moore secured the license number and learned that the

car started out Highway 43 towards Houston. Officers put out a dragnet immediately after the robbery, and officers at Mexia, Athens, Huntsville, Dallas, Fort Worth, Houston, Crockett, Jacksonville, and other places blocked highways and byways.

Three men were held in jail that afternoon as suspects in the daring daylight robbery of the Robinson State Bank that morning. None of the suspects had been identified, and no charges had been filed against them. They were arrested in the downtown district before noon and eventually released, never seriously considered as suspects. The law wanted them for liquor charges and questioning in a robbery concerning the Frankston State Bank.

A fourth suspect in the robbery of the Robinson State Bank was arrested downtown and locked in the county jail at 4:00 P.M. The suspect was nabbed in a southside residence. Two half-gallon jars of alcohol were found at his living quarters. He appeared extremely nervous while being searched before entering a cell. One of the suspects was arrested as he came out of a downtown rooming house shortly before noon. The suspects held in jail were arrested separately. One of them had once been arrested as a suspect in the robbery of the Frankston Bank on December 10, 1930, but was later released. Joel Carroll, Jack Wilson, Billy Belote, and John "Poodle" Hammond later confessed to the Frankston robbery.

Three women had called at the sheriff's office that afternoon and made inquiries concerning the suspects. One of them brought magazines, including *True Detective, Real Detective,* and *True Confessions.* They were not permitted to see the suspects.

Norman J. York would become a familiar name in trying to catch the Whitey Walker Gang. As the manager of the Burns Detective Agency in Houston, he arrived in Palestine that afternoon to take up the investigation of the robbery of the Robinson State Bank. York, who formerly worked in Palestine as a railroad officer, played a prominent part in clearing up an attempted robbery of the First National Bank in Palestine on November 18, 1931. It was York who went to the bank after the robbery and found the loot totaling about $8,000 in a money sack beneath the cashier's window.

Officers began investigating a clue that the bandits might have been members of a gang of Oklahoma outlaws who were known to have been staying recently around Marlin. This gang, some of whom had prison records in Oklahoma State penitentiaries, had been seen in Falls County, according to the *Palestine Daily Herald*.[9]

The robbers had rented a house on Royal Street and had carefully planned the robbery.[10] According to Mrs. Surles,

> There was a woman here in town—her name I'm not certain of—that had rented her rooms to these people. They had come earlier to live here to case the situation, I assume. She was thrilled to rent her rooms. She lived on Royal Street, I think. She told her bridge club that she had rented the rooms to some nice people, and she wanted them to meet them. They never got around to meeting one another.

Mrs. Surles laughed aloud.

Lester Hamilton thought about the old times some more. He moved in his chair some, gave a snort that was probably reserved for someone fifty years ago, and then started talking:

> When the railroad first was built here, they built the station where it is now. That was about a mile from the courthouse. Well, the courthouse was where everything was centered. So to get people moved from the courthouse to what they called downtown, they put in a trolley, a horse-drawn streetcar to run just from downtown to the courthouse, and it didn't last very long. When it went under, they sold the first trolley car or streetcar that Dallas had—sold it to Dallas. I think that Dallas has grown on account of that street car.
>
> Yeah, they had a cotton—Swift had a cotton gin here and the Shelton Gin, there was several. There were four or five of them. Cotton as a cash crop was about the only thing people could grow and get the money right now, which was what they needed. Cotton thrived here and everywhere else in this part of the country, until it became hard to get cotton pickers. People just didn't want to pick cotton for, I don't remember how much they got, something like one dollar for a hundred pounds. It wasn't a very rich undertaking. When they couldn't get pickers anymore, they couldn't grow cotton anymore. It's as simple as that.
>
> There was another robbery, two more robberies of the same bank after it became the First National Bank. The

cashier of the bank was a man named Porter Cooper. Banks at that time could issue currency legally and the bank was robbed by an internal deal. A man who lived out towards the Tennessee Colony here in the county would hold up the bank, hold Porter Cooper up, and then grab the money and run. It worked so well the first time that they pulled it again. Then Porter Cooper was discovered by the law. It was a cinch to rob Porter Cooper because he wanted to be robbed. That was during the '30s too.

Porter Cooper had been issuing all the money, so his name was on the bills that were robbed. They showed up here and there and everywhere. Cooper went to the penitentiary for some years, I don't remember how many. When he got out, those bills began to appear. I had one for a while. Oh, yeah. He bought himself a suit of clothes right away out of that.

Newspaper stories worked a little differently back then. I'll tell you the way that worked. The AP would take the story from us or anybody else and bylines were not very often used in that day. Very seldom were they used. You know the Associated Press so-called membership thing is operated like any other business, but it is advertised as a membership.

We'd send it to them and give it to them and they'd put their own dateline on it. They might change it, edit it, or make a few changes in it, or drop part of it. One paper in town was getting the Associated Press, but the other paper was not, but they were running the same stories that the *Herald* was and they were coming out right away with them. My father one day put out an issue of the *Herald Press* that said, "London Bridge Has Fallen Down," and so sure enough, the other paper came out with this big headline "London Bridge Has Fallen Down."

Of course, they had only run this one paper, and they realized what was happening. They had a kid who would stay down at the *Herald,* and he would grab one of the papers and run back up there with it and then they would print the stories. Well, Pop only printed one or two papers. Then of course they went ahead and printed their papers. That was *The Daily Visitor.*

"London Bridge Has Fallen Down." That was their banner headline. That paper was still in operation for a long time.

"It was, but they didn't run any more Associated Press stories," Frances said.

CHAPTER 5

The Caldwell Jewelry Store Robbery

The town of Bryan is in Brazos County about halfway between Houston and Waco, Texas. The only paved roads in 1933, a luxury for the small towns during the Great Depression, were downtown. Bryan was no different than many other small towns.

There were levels of social stature, a courthouse gang, the business elite—and like other towns where everyone knew everybody else's business, some controversy. There was an area referred to as "Silk Stocking Road," a neighborhood laced with white-columned houses and large porches.

In an age before television and instant digital gratification from a computer, the art of conversation was one of the few ways to pass the little free time available. Money was scarce, and the trolley between Texas A&M College and downtown Bryan could be a costly fare for the people used to doing without. Farms steadily collapsed, and people were forced to move to town and look for any work available. Cotton was still king but for most people no longer very profitable.

General frustration about economic and racial conditions brought about social unrest, and hate groups like the Ku Klux Klan wore white robes proudly at church revival meetings in Brazos County. Some who refused to join were often threatened and ridiculed. This description fits the mold of many other semi-rural towns in a struggling depression.

Mable Doerge describes 1930s Bryan, Texas:

Years ago, everybody, especially country people, would dress and go to town on Saturday afternoon. Maybe just sit in the car and watch people, or maybe we would have some shopping to do, because we didn't go to town too often. Even though we lived here and everything, we didn't go too often. That was a weekend spree.

My cousin used to run that trolley car to downtown. All the roads out towards Kurten and Reliance, where I lived, were nothing but just old dirt roads. In fact, when it rained, there was a hill that they couldn't get over around Steep Hollow. You didn't, you just didn't, come to town when it was wet and rainy.

Cotton and corn. Honey, I've chopped many a row of cotton and many a row of corn. And my Daddy, he was a person, he was one of these types that he got up and hit his fields, and we would always—there was six of us children, three boys and three girls—and we'd work our fields out and have it clean and then we were free to go help other people. Course, they paid us for working in the field, chopping cotton, or thinning corn, or whatever.

Mrs. Easter taught school at Reliance, Texas, in a one-room school with a wood burning stove. People carried their lunch in a paper bag. I remember the old watering trough down on the north end of Bryan where people used to take their animals. They would come to town in the wagons and buggies or whatever you had. They used this big round water trough down at the north end of Main Street where they would go and water their animals. It was just a big old round tank with water flowing where people would go and water their animals. Well, I've been here a long time.

When the crash hit around here, everything dropped. The farmers all failed, the crops failed, there were no crops made. I remember, of course, I wasn't anything except just a young person then, that there were no crops, no cotton, no corn. Everything was gone. That dry year, my mother had a sister that lived in Comanche, and we had an old Ford touring car. Daddy loaded us all up and we'd go to Comanche and pick cotton.

There was no money to be had and we did without mostly. A bunch of us worked at the laundry and was glad to get it. It didn't pay but $55 a month, but $55 was a lot of money back in those times.

Not everyone was content with riding out the worst of the Great Depression. Robbery and gang activity thrived in the big cities, and by 1933, members of the Barrow Gang were household names. Small-town banks that had not collapsed due to the economy had to worry about daylight armed robberies from thieves who were often armed with automatic weapons stolen from national armories. The Browning Automatic Rifle (BAR) was a heavy, cumbersome, World War I weapon, but with a twenty-round clip and bullets that could punch through armor, it was the weapon of choice for many Texas outlaws.

It seemed as though every time that there was another armed robbery anywhere in the South or Midwest, it had to have been Bonnie and Clyde, or at least Ray Hamilton. If the Barrow Gang had been involved in even a fraction of the cases attributed to them, they would have had to magically appear all over the country. While the police were pursuing false leads of the Barrow Gang, other equally desperate groups were making headlines. Now forgotten, partially due to the legacy of the 1967 movie *Bonnie and Clyde,* these other desperado groups were making daring raids across the nation. One of the most dangerous of these forgotten gangs was the Whitey Walker Gang.

It was unusually warm in Bryan on Thursday, December 14, 1933. The high temperature was 82 degrees, and the low would not quite reach 60 degrees that winter day. John Sealey Caldwell and his wife, Celeste, were ready to close their jewelry store for the day at around 6:15 P.M. Business had been brisk since the Caldwells had been advertising a Christmas sale throughout the month in the local newspaper.

At 6:30 P.M., closing time, Mr. and Mrs. Caldwell left the jewelry store. "As we went out the back door, these men swung around in the middle of the block," Mrs. Caldwell stated, "and someone yelled, 'We want you.'"

John Sealey asked, "What do you want?"

"We want what you got," he replied.

Mr. Caldwell said that he had just locked his store and was walking to the curb to enter his car when a man stepped up, grabbed him by one arm, and shoved a gun against his ribs. Mrs. Caldwell, who was at the curb, was treated in a similar fashion.[2]

The three men forced Mr. and Mrs. Caldwell to return to the Bryan Avenue entrance and told Mr. Caldwell to unlock the door. Once in the store, the Caldwells were marched to the safe, which Mr. Caldwell, still menaced by the revolvers of the three bandits, was told to open. He had no choice but to open the safe.

Celeste Caldwell continued her account of what happened: "After unlocking the back door, we went to the old safe. They wouldn't let John turn on the lights, but struck matches on the safe to give him light to dial the combination of the safe." Being nervous and trying to open the safe by the flickering matches made it difficult for Mr. Caldwell to open it. Cash from the day's sale, diamond rings, other diamond-set jewelry, and all the valuable watches were taken from the safe. The safe was completely looted.[3] Losses were thought to be between $8,000 and $10,000.[4]

After the loot had been gathered up and put in a sack, the three men ordered Mr. and Mrs. Caldwell to accompany them to their car, a small four-door sedan, and enter it on Bryan Avenue. "It was the first Ford V-8. John Sealey and I were bundled into the back along with Blackie Thompson," said Mrs. Caldwell. According to Mr. Caldwell, the driver acted drunk as he drove the car north on Bryan Avenue and out Highway 21. After they had passed Kurten, the driver took the road to the small town of Edge. He drove for about a mile and a half and then stopped the car. The Caldwells were told to get out of the vehicle, which they did, and they were marched about a hundred yards into a thicket.[5]

"After we took off, the thieves began to speak in 'Dog Latin,' which we of course could understand. Using this technique they said that they would take us to the other side of Kurten," Mrs. Caldwell said.

The little Ford V-8 turned on the first road to the left and crossed the creek. The robbers took the Caldwells from the car and led them away from the road. Mrs. Caldwell was having a hard time walking in her high heels. They came to a gully they had to jump across. "Roy Johnson, the only one that had been nice to me, told them that I couldn't jump to the other side," said Mrs. Caldwell.

After being helped across, the robbers forced the arms of each of their victims behind them and tied their arms around a tree. "They proceeded to tie us with their dirty handkerchiefs," Mrs. Caldwell stated with a disgusted look. The robbers also tied their thumbs together with copper wire.[6] Then they were forced to sit on a log, to which they were bound by more wire. Their captors then left. Both Mr. and Mrs. Caldwell set to work to free themselves. Wire cut Mrs. Caldwell's hands before she managed to get free and release Mr. Caldwell. About thirty minutes had passed since the robbers left. The Caldwells started to walk toward Highway 21. After reaching the road, they attempted to flag down a number of motorists, who refused to stop. They walked about two miles toward Kurten, where they were picked up by an insurance man named Clifton Steen. The group first stopped at Kurten to telephone Sheriff J. H. Reed about the robbery before they were brought back to Bryan.

About an hour after the robbery, E. R. Canady, who was returning from Madisonville, reported that a car being driven at a high rate of speed in the direction of Bryan had passed him about seven miles out. Police believed this was the car of the robbers, and that the criminals had doubled back to Bryan in an effort to throw possible pursuers off their trail. They believed that three men were in the car and estimated the speed at about seventy-five miles per hour. Mr. Canady and another man named Roy Vick were riding together and saw no license tag.[7]

Later that night, Mr. and Mrs. Caldwell found themselves in separate rooms of the Houston Police Department looking through mug shots to identify the men who had robbed them. After a short time, each of the Caldwells identified the same men that robbed their store. These men, known as the Whitey Walker Gang, were characterized as dangerous and vicious gangsters known to associate with other criminals such as Raymond Hamilton, Bonnie Parker, and Clyde Barrow. On their return to Bryan, the Caldwells were put up in a local hotel for fear that the gang would return and make good their promise to harm anyone who told on them. The Caldwells spent several months at the hotel.[8]

Police of the city and county scoured the country during the night and sent out an alarm to various cities of the state. Three men were arrested by Houston police, in a car carrying a Maryland license, but after they had been seen by Mr. and Mrs. Caldwell, they were released.[9]

The robbers had seemed to know that Mr. Caldwell planned to leave by the Bryan Avenue door as they lay in wait for him and Mrs. Caldwell. Mr. Caldwell thought that all three men, who were of middle age, were strangers to him and he had no recollection of ever having had seen them before the night of the robbery.[10]

Investigations by local police officials following the holdup of the Caldwells and the looting of the safe indicated that three men and two women spent several days in Bryan before the holdup and kidnapping. The chief of police, K. T. Tiflis, believed that the gang lived for several days in a rent house owned by B. F. Parks, located to the rear of his home on Baker Avenue.

It was believed that the three men left Bryan at about 11:00 P.M. and that the two women left the following morning. The police had a description of the two cars that were used by the gang while in Bryan, and a search of the house disclosed boxes and some silverware identified as having come from the Caldwell store.[11]

Several days passed, and there was still no indication of the whereabouts of the gang. Bryan police chief Tiflis received another call from some disturbed people near the intersection of College Avenue (the present Texas Avenue) and 31st Street. They told the chief to come over right then, that the suspicious people had left the house on Baker Street they had rented since December 1 from Mr. B. F. Parks. The previous calls from the concerned citizens had obviously fallen on deaf ears. The chief told officers Howard Lee and J. W. Hamilton about the latest call but failed to mention the previous calls. The officers were sent to the house to investigate the complaint.[12]

Officer Lee said, "We went down there, and when we walked in—we knew that there was a gang in town. It was a hideout. Dirty dishes and everything—you know, and they were all gone." The neighbors indicated there were two women with the three men. They became suspicious when it was noticed that meals were being delivered to the house from a local restaurant. Also, the postman was told not to come to the house because they wouldn't be receiving any mail.

After investigating the house used as a hideout, the officers called the police department in Houston to send someone to help take fingerprints and identify the past occupants. It took the Houston investigators about twenty minutes to determine that it was the Whitey Walker Gang that had occupied the small house.[13]

One interesting story regarding the gang's brief and mysterious stay in Bryan revolves around their love for Coca-Cola. A few doors down from the Baker Street hideout was a gasoline service station. At that station was a soft drink machine, the old mechanical kind where a person would lift the lid and the bottles were held vertically by their necks. To get a bottled soft drink, a person would put money in and slide the bottle down a rack to be released at the end of the row. The gang apparently loved these drinks, and oftentimes they could be found sitting out in front of this service station smoking cigarettes and sipping on a bottle of Coca-Cola. If anyone asked them what they were doing in town, they replied that they were thinking about opening a business in town, maybe a garage.[14]

The story goes that the day after the Caldwell robbery the soft drink distributor came to the station to collect money and restock the machine. What he found instead was an empty machine—empty of soft drinks, that is, because the bottles were still in the machine. It appeared that someone had lifted the lid, popped the tops off the bottles, and drank the contents with a straw while the bottles were still on the rack. The gang had disappeared and couldn't be asked about the incident.[15] If this was the work of the Whitey Walker Gang, it is strange behavior for men who had already robbed at least two banks for thousands of dollars to be too cheap to pay for their own Cokes. Tales like this are not all that unusual, however. Members of the Barrow Gang were known to rob a place and then go out of their way to steal gas at a Ma and Pa gas station while on the run from the police. Maybe it was just the thrill of getting away with something that led them to commit these petty crimes.

Sam Fling worked for the Caldwells as a jeweler for over forty years. He recalls the conversation he had with Mr. Caldwell regarding the Whitey Walker Gang robbery:

> Caldwell Jewelers was a long store. It went from one street to the other, you know. It went all the way through, and it had those tall sides, where they had Mrs. Caldwell's silver and stuff like that on one side. She had dishes on the other side, china

dishes. There was a repair shop right in the back, and it had the safe back there. Customers could walk in from Main Street or the other street, either one. They could come in from either way. I guess fifty percent of our customers come back through the back door. They could see everything.

The safe was sitting out in the open. It was a big old safe. It was about as tall as I am and had about, I think it had three of those old knobs sticking out on it. You know, where the doors opened up. The doors opened on both sides. I opened that thing a whole lot.

Right above the repair shop, John Sealy had a little old room there. Every Christmas, about the time when you wanted a drink of whiskey, you could just go back there and get you a drink. He had all them people coming in for Christmas, you know. Shoot, man, they'd come in there and take that bottle and pours them a little sip, put it back down and go on.

John Sealey was a good man. He'd just trust them people who'd want a ring. He'd sell it to them, boy. Lots of times, if you wanted to gamble . . . well, that's another story.

John Sealy told me they come right in closing time, you know, so there wouldn't be any more people coming in, but they didn't have no way to block that view. Shades are pulled down today from one end to the other. It was just open, just a door there, and there was a glass window back there where we repaired. You could see right off that street into the repair shop. It was a glass window—it opened all the way, and you could see from that window all the way through the store.

They had a pretty good payroll, you know. He said they took all their money. Then he said that they took them out in the woods somewhere toward Kurten, and they tied them up out there. And that's when that man noticed Mrs. Caldwell didn't have no rings on, and that's when they got mad.

Mrs. Caldwell knew something was wrong, she just knew they was going to rob them, and she slipped her rings off and just dropped them on the floor behind where she was standing, behind the counter. And that's what made them mad when they got out there. She didn't have no rings. She known good and well they'd probably cased the store, because she known good and well she had a pretty good-sized diamond, and she wore it all the time.

One of them said they were going to kill them. They were going to shoot them. John said they had that pistol out. Boy, they were ready.

'You don't talk to the boy no more!' one of them said to Mrs.
Caldwell [referring to her talking to Roy Johnson, who was the
youngest of the gang]. But the other guy spoke up. You know,
they never did kill nobody, and he didn't want to be on that
death rap. John says they turned around and walked off. Left
them tied behind that tree. Said they tied their hands behind
that tree with wire. I never did ask him how in the world they
ever got undone. He's lucky, I tell you what. He said he was
lucky. He was a fine fellow. Never could work with nobody better, I can guarantee.[16]

The Whitey Walker Gang still had much to do before they
were captured. After a successful escape from Bryan, the gang
set its eyes on the First State Bank of Marlin. The gang had
Dolores Walker with them to set up a hideout before the robbery. Sometimes a second, unknown woman would accompany
the group as they traveled across the state.

The unusual style of the gang that set them apart from
other noted outlaws lay in how they conducted their robberies.
If they robbed a bank, they would usually force everyone into
the vault but would instruct the prisoners how to release themselves. This task would be time consuming for the victims and
would allow the gang a clean getaway.

The only people not in the vault would be the hostages that
the Whitey Walker Gang would take with them during an
escape. They seemed to take hostages whether they needed
them as shields or not.

Another interesting action taken by the gang involved how
the hostages were tied when left in an isolated spot. The hostages would be told to keep their heads down and their eyes
closed, and the gang would tie the victims' thumbs together with
either copper or fencing wire. More wire would then be used to
tie the victims to a tree or a log. If the hostages did not do exactly what they were told, Thompson made it clear that it would be
"Too bad for you," as he showed his pistol as an explanation of
his intent.

The headlines in *The Bryan Daily Eagle* on December 15 and
16, 1933, would paint the Whitey Walker Gang as a group to be
feared in the same way Bonnie and Clyde's names struck terror
in the population. There would be a new headline in less than
two weeks—this time in Marlin, Texas.

CHAPTER 6

On to Marlin

All the mineral baths are gone these days. Even the ruins of the old bath houses have been obliterated so that progress could continue in Marlin, Texas. At one time, though, the bath houses were the heart of Marlin's tourist and healing industry. Marlin is located in Falls County, named after a small waterfall in the nearby Brazos River.

While many towns were reeling from an ailing cotton market, Marlin was the place to be in 1933. There were grand hotels, sanitariums, and the secret magic of the hot artesian water so rich in minerals that it was supposed to cleanse the body of impurities. Claiming to cure everything from blood disease to gonorrhea, there was no shortage of patrons ready for a quick and natural cure for their ailments. Names such as the Majestic Bath House, Torbett's Sanitorium Clinic, and the Crippled Children's Hospital and Exercising Pool graced the downtown area. Hotels such as the Falls and the Majestic boasted of multi-story buildings offering over a hundred rooms each to accommodate those patrons willing to pay. So that a patient didn't have to get out of bathing attire, there was an underground corridor that led from the hotels to their chosen institution of wonder—not too bad for an industry that went from a 3,000-foot-deep bad town water well in 1893 to a fifty-foot, 147-degree, money-making geyser.

V. M. Bradshaw was the vice president of the First State Bank in Marlin, Texas. At fifty-seven years of age, he was quite active and was used to doing work that called for him to be awake and downtown early. Besides being a bank vice president, he helped his sons deliver newspapers. One son was an agent for the *Dallas News,* and Bradshaw would help the boys deliver the papers all over town at daylight. He had not missed a morning doing that task for about five years. He started working at the First State Bank in September 1909; prior to that time, his position was the district clerk from 1906 to 1910.[1]

On December 27, 1933, Bradshaw was at the bank, but he didn't get to do any work. He arrived at the bank that morning at about 7:15 A.M. He usually got to the bank that early. He didn't drive his car because he usually walked to work. When he came down the street in the vicinity of the bank on that particular morning, there was nothing out of the ordinary; he did notice the two or three cars stopped by the restaurant, and three or four cars parked along Main Street. However, there was nothing unusual about that. Bradshaw noticed two people in one car; the car was sitting in front of the Home Benefit Association, which is the second door to the east of the bank. From his room in the Falls Hotel, immediately north of the alley behind the bank, Whitey Hatcher was quoted later as telling authorities that he saw an automobile with four people wearing caps near the bank. Bradshaw went to the front door of the bank on Main Street. The door was locked when he got there, and he unlocked it and started to walk in, when something unusual happened. After passing inside the entrance to the bank, someone pushed him inside with their body. Thinking it was some boy or a friend who had just pushed in, the bank vice president looked up and said, "Hello."

He saw it was not a friend. It was Blackie Thompson. The outlaw didn't say anything for a minute. Bradshaw made a remark to him, then looked up at him, and down again, and saw his gun. Thompson had a pistol; he had it in his right hand next to his hip. The banker didn't know what kind of gun it was. At that point, another man walked into the bank.

"I will go back out," the second man said, and then he left.

When Bradshaw saw the gun, he raised his hands. Thompson told him to put his hands down, that he was not going to hurt him. Then he walked up and pulled the shades down on the door. "I haven't got any money. I have a dollar or two in my pocket, and a dollar or two on the desk is all I have," Bradshaw told Thompson.

"Four of us are here working on this job. We've been here three or four days, and we know all the surroundings," replied Thompson.[2] "Have you got a burglar alarm?" he continued.

"No," Bradshaw said.

"Do you have any tear gas?" Thompson asked, apparently remembering the Palestine fiasco.

"No."

Thompson then let Bradshaw know that it would be too bad for him if he tried to fool the outlaw. He told the banker to open the vault and, whatever he did, try not to touch anything with his hands or feet. It is probable that the outlaw was concerned about alarm switches. Then he motioned for Bradshaw to start moving and open the vault. Bradshaw turned the combination and threw one bolt.

"Unscrew the door," Thompson barked.

Bradshaw did; Thompson was standing at the banker's left side at the time.

"Come on back up here," said Thompson, and watched Bradshaw walk near the teller's window. Thompson pulled the stool up, pulled Bradshaw's hat off, and then got a little to the back of the banker to his left. Bradshaw sat there about fifteen or twenty minutes until about 7:30. It was at this point that a porter came into the bank. Thompson had the porter lay face down on the floor at Bradshaw's feet. Someone came in, possibly the little news boy, Pat Rojas. Bradshaw couldn't look around because his back was towards the door.

"I think that is the news boy," Thompson remarked.

Around 7:35, Mr. Spencer came by with the mail, and as was his usual custom, he said, "Good morning, Mr. Bradshaw."

"Hello, Shaw."[3]

Shaw Spencer lived in Marlin, and his occupation was that of a letter carrier. His duties included carrying mail to the First State Bank. On the morning of December 27, Spencer went to the bank. He saw Bradshaw and then Thompson. Blackie

Thompson was standing by Mr. Bradshaw's side when Spencer first saw him. The tone of Bradshaw's voice gave Spencer a chill —he was a moment slower to start talking than when he usually replied, and, being a little bit uneasy, the letter carrier wanted him to say a little something else.

"It looks like we are going to have some bad weather," Spencer said as he laid down the mail on Bradshaw's desk. Thompson was coming around into Bradshaw's office. Thompson came to where Spencer was and took up the conversation immediately. As Thompson walked up to Mr. Bradshaw's desk, he picked up the *Dallas News* and was talking to Spencer over the newspaper.[4]

"It does look like we are going to have some bad weather— it looks like it's going to snow." His attitude towards Spencer was very friendly.

When Spencer left there, he was not satisfied everything was all right, but he just talked himself out of making a report about it.[5] That chill feeling was not enough to report the situation to officers. The fact that Mr. Thompson was so nice and friendly and that he didn't stop Spencer left a doubt in his mind—possibly he was mistaken.

Bradshaw told Thompson, "That man used to live right across the street from me, and he is suspicious of any incident or things, and the chances are he will have the entire sheriff's department in here in fifteen minutes."

"If he does, it will be too bad for us," was Thompson's reply.

Just before Thompson left for the front door, he asked Bradshaw to give him his keys. Bradshaw complied, and Thompson then asked about the key to the back door. Bradshaw told him the key to the back door was in the door, that it stayed there. If not, there was one on his desk. Another man came in and spoke about the key, and Bradshaw told him the same thing—that the key was in the back door. "Don't fool me or double cross me," the man said. The other man was Whitey Walker.[6]

Miss Andrew Peyton also lived in Marlin and worked at the First State Bank as a bookkeeper.[7] She usually got to the bank at 8:30 A.M., but on the day of the robbery she got there at 8:00 or a very few minutes thereafter. Miss Peyton had been working in the bank since 1920. She came from Oltorf and Kyser's and went to the bank downtown. Oltorf and Kyser's was a grocery store that was located on Main Street in Marlin, about two blocks from the courthouse, and the First State Bank was located on the north side of Main Street in the third block from the courthouse.[8]

When Miss Peyton entered the bank from the Main Street entrance, the only bank employees already there were Mr. Bradshaw and Lee Humphrey, the bank porter. She entered through a door to the left and came through the banker's office. Lee Humphrey was lying on the floor. Bradshaw was sitting on the stool, and Thompson was standing at Bradshaw's back. Miss Peyton had not seen Thompson prior to the time she noticed Lee and the bank executive. As she came through the door, she was looking at the porter. Thompson came from around Bradshaw and grabbed Miss Peyton's arm. As she tried to pull away, he put his other arm around her. She was still trying to pull away when she got to where Bradshaw could catch her arm and pull her away from Thompson. They stood there, and Thompson stood right by them. Someone came from the back after a few minutes, through a side door. As he came through this door, Miss Peyton looked up.

"Don't you look," the man said.

When she looked a second time, he said, "God damn you, if you look again, I'll shoot you." The man who said that was Whitey Walker.[9] As Bradshaw looked around, he saw that Thompson was unfolding a sack made out of ducking. He pulled it out of his pocket, and Bradshaw immediately realized what it was for. Walker came in and said, "We had better complete the job. People outside are getting excited—I saw a car running up the street in a hurry."

"Come on in the vault," Thompson told Bradshaw.

The banker had told him that he didn't know the combination to the safe that was inside the vault. The vault had a large door, and a person could walk through the door of the vault to the safe. The safe that was inside the vault had a combination and time lock. Bradshaw told him that he didn't know the combination; Mr. McKinely, the cashier, had that.

"When Mr. McKinely gets here, I am going to ask if that's so, and if it is not, it will be too bad for you," Thompson told Bradshaw.[10]

"We know that you know the combination to this safe, and if you don't open it, it will be too bad," Thompson continued. Bradshaw decided to open the safe, hoping all the time that as he was turning the combination, it would not work. The banker could see that the men were getting nervous.

Bradshaw unlocked the safe. He worked on the combination, having to get down on a knee to do so. When he got back up, Thompson said, "Unscrew the door."

After the safe was opened, Bradshaw was taken back to where the porter and Miss Peyton were, back to the stool where he had been sitting. Thompson instructed him to stay there. Thompson went back to the vault, and Bradshaw watched what the bandits were doing by looking through a ventilation hole cut in the wall between his office and the vault. Walker was taking the money out of the safe, and Thompson was holding the sack and holding the pistol in his hand. When the banker looked at the outlaws, Thompson stood up, still holding the sack. The banker looked the other way.

In a short time they came out with the money. Walker had the money and securities, and Thompson came back to the bank employees. "Let's go," Thompson told them.

Thompson took Miss Peyton's arm and said, "We are going."

The group went to the back of the bank—the robbers told Bradshaw and Lee Humphrey to take the money, and Miss Peyton was led out the back door of the bank. Walker was in front, and Thompson was still behind Bradshaw. Walker told Bradshaw to take the two sacks of silver. Thompson was still behind the banker when the group went to the car, which was parked in the back of the bank. Bradshaw and Humphrey were told to get in the back seat, and Thompson got in the back seat with Bradshaw. Lee was in the middle and Thompson was on his right side with Walker driving the car.[11] The engine of the car was running, and one of the robbers ordered the bookkeeper to get in the front seat. Walker grabbed her, and he told the bookkeeper to get in the car, which she did. Miss Peyton did not talk to the robbers after she got in the car.[12]

The Whitey Walker Gang stole $44,141.70 in money and securities belonging to the bank, including $7,000 worth of lib-

erty bonds and $8,300 in other bonds that belonged to cus-
tomers. The gang got some jewelry: two rings, a small inexpen-
sive watch (which was returned in a note case), a brooch, and
some kind of a button. They also took an old piece of jewelry
that had been in the family of a customer for thirty-five years.[13]
The common estimate of the theft is listed as $41,000, but Brad-
shaw related the higher figure to authorities. Why the figure was
rounded off to a lower amount for the newspapers is unknown.

A newspaper article written for *The Daily Democrat* on
December 28, 1933, in Marlin described what happened next.
(Official transcripts as well as newspapers of this time period
usually specify if a person involved is of a race other than white.
I take the liberty as the author to write what has been recorded
so as to not bias the evidence. Although the intentionally racist
dialogue is abhorrent by today's standards, it is nonetheless a
true reflection of events during the Great Depression and cap-
tures the atmosphere of the Marlin bank robbery):

> Lee Humphrey, Marlin negro employed as a porter at the
> First State Bank and kidnaped along with M. V. Bradshaw, Sr.,
> and Miss Andrew Peyton, bookkeeper, when the place was
> robbed Wednesday morning, now knows all about bandits, and
> likely won't be so inquisitive if he ever has contact with them
> again.
>
> When Lee walked into the robber trap at the bank on
> reporting for duty Wednesday morning, he didn't at first real-
> ize what it was all about. As he entered the lobby and started
> down the corridor toward the rear of the bank, Lee was accost-
> ed with the command, "Stop, there!"
>
> Peering through a teller window and seeing the man was
> a stranger, Lee said, "What does ah wanta stop fuh?"
>
> "Come on around here," was the next order from the
> bandit.
>
> And Lee, still wondering what was going on, decided he
> would ask another.
>
> "What does ah wanta come 'round there fuh?"
>
> "Come on around here, Lee," Mr. Bradshaw told the
> porter, who then complied.
>
> When the vault was opened, Lee was made a bearer of
> burdens, being given three sacks of silver to transport to the
> car. However, because it was a little too much of a load, or for
> some other reason entirely satisfactory to himself, Lee left one

of the sacks on the table in the rear of the bank where it was found on discovery of the robbery.

The car was in the alley facing east, and the robbers and hostages drove out of the alley to Railroad Street and then to the garage on the corner, and turned back west on Coleman Street. After they passed the post office and before they got to the corner, the car turned north on Ward Street. Thompson had Bradshaw's keys.

"If you don't mind, give me those keys. They will be of no service to you, and it would cause me lots of trouble," the banker told the robbers.

"God damn you, they will not be of any service to you, unless you shut your eyes, we'll jab them out," was Walker's reply.

Bradshaw then kept his eyes shut most of the time. Inside the car, Bradshaw noticed two guns. He thought one was an automatic "pump gun" and the other a repeating rifle—he did not know the make of them. The car had not gone a mile or so when Walker asked Thompson if he had gotten the guns out, and he said, "Yes."[14]

It was a cold, cloudy day. Miss Peyton became disoriented as to where they were driving. She did not know what direction they took or traveled as the vehicle left town, because after the carload of outlaws and hostages turned the corner at the Home Oil Company, Walker told Miss Peyton to close her eyes if she knew what was good for her. The woman put her hands up over her eyes. "If I were you, I'd take my hands down," Walker remarked. Miss Peyton put her hands down and kept her eyes closed all day.[15] She supposed it was about 8:15 or 8:20 when they left town, and between 10:00 and 11:00 before the car finally stopped.[16]

Discovery of the robbery was made by S. L. Golding, a Marlin cotton buyer, who said he went into the bank at about 8:15 A.M. People were guessing at the exact time of events, but it was certain that the escape of the bandits and discovery of the robbery were very close. Finding the interior apparently arranged for the beginning of the day's business and no one in it, Golding, after a hurried survey of the situation and noting a money sack on a table, rushed to the street and gave the alarm.

W. F. McKinley, a cashier at the bank, also apparently missed the robbery by only a short time, as he arrived at the place a few minutes after it was discovered.

The getaway car was uncomfortable. The outlaws had a metal tire cover in the car, and both Humphrey and Bradshaw had to put their feet up on the tire cover. Thompson had no tire cover, but he sat on the edge of the seat, and that tire cover made riding very uncomfortable.[17]

It was around two and a half to three hours from the time the getaway car left Marlin to the time the car stopped somewhere in the countryside. About the only conversation on the trip between the hostages and the kidnappers was when Bradshaw conveyed his realization of the danger they were all in if they were seen. Bradshaw told Thompson that if they went through some little town and some officer spotted them, it would be dangerous.

"Yes, dangerous for all of us," remarked Thompson. Actually, the fear was a realistic one, because authorities throughout the area were requested to keep a lookout on highways and roads for the suspected car. Walker asked a time or two if Thompson saw the other car, and Thompson would look back and say, "I think I see it coming."

This happened two or three times during the trip. One time Walker said he saw a motorcycle, and they were concerned about that and finally said they thought it was a mail carrier—they didn't understand this motorcycle.[18]

The group crossed the Brazos River on the Belton bridge. The roads were rough; it didn't seem like they were driving on the highway. The roads were also not straight for any distance, at least for long. The robbers seemed bothered about which road to take. One time Walker wanted to miss some road work, and Bradshaw couldn't tell whether he missed it or not. At other times Walker thought he was not on the right road, and sometimes he would have to change directions.

M. V. Bradshaw Jr., son of the kidnapped vice president of the bank, returned from Dallas that afternoon after having driven all the way to the city that morning. There was a report that a car similar to the one seen in the alley had run a red light in Waco and headed toward Dallas. However, the trail of the car

was lost. It was said to have been occupied by several men, including a negro.

It was very cold that day. When Walker stopped the car, the
robbers told the hostages they would have to stay in the car until
night. Both thieves then got out of the car, and Miss Peyton only
saw Blackie Thompson two times the rest of the day. They did-
n't take the hostages out of the car when they stopped; they all
stayed together and sat in the car all day.[19]

The captives were told to stay in the car while the two robbers got out and built a fire. The robbers drank whiskey as long
as their supply lasted and appeared to regret when there was
none left. They also smoked, one of them consuming cigarettes
incessantly one after another during the trip and at the pasture,
appearing to be very nervous (again a recurring scene in all the
robberies).

The bank vice president could hear the robbers talking a little. He didn't know what they were doing. He heard a noise, and
it had a metallic sound. At different times the thieves would pass
by the car. The banker would hear the door open; he didn't
know whether maybe it was Miss Peyton or Lee. All three of the
hostages sat in the car. In the meantime, sheriffs, marshals, and
other officers and citizens were scouring the state for all possible clues.

Miss Peyton didn't know where Walker and Thompson
were while they were sitting in the car. Every once in a while she
could hear them, sounds like papers rattling, and then something popping. She didn't know whether it was a bradding
machine, a gun, or what. The hostages stayed in the car until it
was just beginning to get dark. "It was cold, but they gave us
blankets," the bookkeeper later told authorities.[20]

When the hostages got out of the car they had no idea just
what time it was. It must have been around 6:30 P.M.[21] When they
took Bradshaw and Humphrey out, the bookkeeper broke down
crying. Whitey Walker took Bradshaw out of the car first, and
they were gone with him about five or ten minutes before they
came back to the vehicle. It was sprinkling a drop or two.

"I ought to knock you off. You have been trying to peep all
day," Walker said to the banker. Bradshaw told Walker, "I have
not been trying to peep, but sitting there with my eyes closed

and my head down, and a couple of times I put my hat this way, but I was not trying to peep; but my neck was almost broken holding my head down for eight or ten hours. Well, you can hurt me, you can bump me off, but I have not peeped at you."[22]

"You can look up now; it's all right," the bandit replied. "Where are we?" was the reply.

Bradshaw saw two boys tied to trees as he and Whitey passed by them. Walker said he didn't know himself where they were, but these boys knew and would get them out. During the day, two youths came along on a hunting expedition. After the robbers had briefly discussed this turn of events, they decided to tie up the boys and did so, holding them captive with the bank employees until their departure. It was around 10:30 A.M. when the two boys stumbled into the wrong thicket at the wrong time and were captured by the bank robbers. Bradshaw took a closer look and saw that the boys had their backs to the trees and had gags in their mouths. Walker then tied the banker to a small tree by putting his hands behind the tree and tying his thumbs together with copper wire. Walker put a gag in Bradshaw's mouth; the gag was made of paper and cloth and tied with copper wire. The outlaw tied the banker near the two boys.[23] He went back to get Humphrey and tied him the same way near the other bound captives.

Miss Peyton did not know where they were taking her co-workers or what they were doing with them. The bookkeeper had her eyes closed and didn't know whether they had knocked the banker off or done something else to him.[24] Then the robbers came and took Lee; after that, they came for Miss Peyton. She still had her eyes closed, and as the woman got out of the car, they told her that she could open her eyes but to keep her head down. Miss Peyton was crying.

"I thought you said if we did what you said, you would not hurt us," she said to one of the robbers.

The robber said he was not going to hurt her but to keep her mouth shut. "You will not have to stay all night. Some boys will be there to turn you loose," he told her.

When they carried Miss Peyton out, they put her arms behind her and her back against a tree. A gang member then wired her thumbs together from behind, with the tree between her and more wire. Then she was gagged with a big rag stuffed into her mouth. The rag was then wired around her head. She did not see Bradshaw until after they tied her to the tree and gagged her. It is not clear when, but at some point before Bradshaw was gagged, he saw that Walker still had the old note case where the bank kept the real estate notes. The bank vice president then asked Walker to give the case back to him. Walker indicated to him that he would if he looked through it and there was nothing he wanted. Bradshaw thought the group was down around Rockdale judging from the length of time and a train whistle he could hear in the distance. In reality, the group was about seventy miles from their home in Marlin.

"I just have one or two dollars in my pocket, and there are three of us," the banker told Walker when the robber brought the note case back.

"Yes, I will give you some money." He took some money out of his pocket and dropped five fifty-cent pieces in Bradshaw's right-hand pocket.

"Is there anything of any value to us?" the gang leader asked, referring to the note case.

Bradshaw told him no; they would have to foreclose in Marlin, and it would give him a lot of trouble if the robber destroyed it. Walker gave the case back to the banker and also the small watch of little value. Overall, less than ten dollars and two city bonds came back in the case.

"This is something about the city, and you may take it back," Walker said once he was finished with the case.[25] Walker, when he was ready to leave after he had gotten the hostages all tied to the trees and gagged, stopped and said, "Be careful who you identify."

Before they left, Walker said, "You can get loose after we are gone, but don't try to get loose until five minutes after we are gone, and then these boys can get you."[26]

Bradshaw saw that they were in a thicket near the road. When asked later why he kept his eyes closed, Bradshaw remarked, "They said if we didn't keep our eyes closed, they would jab them out or shoot us."

The captives found no difficulty in extricating themselves, and one of the boys ran for help. It was then that the information was relayed to Marlin that all were safe, thanks to a long-distance telephone message from the home of Sam Dolehite of the Val Verde community, the only phone in the area.

Mrs. Violet Dolehite has seen a lot of years near Rogers. When talking to her in 1999, one could feel a strength hidden behind her eighty-five-year-old eyes. She had been a widow for over twenty years. When she wasn't teaching school, she was on horseback, keeping the cattle in check on the ranch while her husband Sam laid irrigation pipe on their spread of over thirty years near the Val Verde community. Even during the terrible drought of the 1950s, the couple kept the ranch from going under like so many others around them. The Dolehites would milk the cows and sell the big cans of separated cream in town on Saturday mornings.

She wanted to retire from teaching in 1940, but with the war taking shape a year later, schoolteachers were hard to come by, so she juggled teaching with the ranch duties. One event that stays in her memory is the Christmas holiday in 1933. That was when Sam, then her fiancé, answered the door of his parents' house to the frantic knocking of a cold young man with a pressing message. Sam relayed the events of that night to his wife, and this is her story:

> The two Davis boys were going out to hunt opossums or armadillos, and I assume they didn't have anything, maybe a .22 caliber gun, and the boys run up on the robbers. The bank robbers kept the boys there the rest of day until late that afternoon. Then they tied them to the trees, also.
>
> He told that they were counting the money and doing things of that sort. They were smoking ready-rolled cigarettes. That really made an impression on those Davis boys, you know, that they had ready-made cigarettes. They wanted one of those ready-made cigarettes so bad they could taste it. At least one of those boys did. Finally, they let them roll a cigarette of their own. But they didn't give them any of their ready rolled. They let them roll one of their own, but they wouldn't give them a ready-made one.
>
> Anyway, one of them got loose after the robbers left. I imagine they probably intended that he do that. When he got loose then, of course, he untied the others. The robbers left, but they had them tied to the trees. It was still a little light. The

boys could see how to get around. It wasn't completely night. I'm sure it was by the time that the young man got here to pick up his father. I'm sure it was night then. Then the Davis boy went up to my husband's father's house to use the telephone. Yes, that one Davis boy that untied the others walked up to the Dolehite house and told Sam about it. So then Sam called to Marlin and talked to Mr. Bradshaw's son.

Everyone was hunting for them and had no idea where to look. I'm sure they had hunted Rogers out, but of course they didn't find anything here. I'm sure that Bryan Walker was pretty familiar with the countryside all around. Anyway, my husband said the lady was pretty well shook up, too. Seems that Mr. Bradshaw had kept pretty calm. My husband's sister was a registered nurse, and I think that helped to calm the lady some.

My husband's father was named Walter. Walter Dolehite. Mr. Dolehite was sick at that time, and he died about a year later of cancer. So, Sam took the car down there and got them and carried them in to Rogers. I was teaching school at Val Verde at the time. I lived during the week with the families in the Val Verde community, and then I would come home on the weekends. My uncle Tom White was postmaster, and he had a car, so he'd come get me and bring me home for the weekend.

I know what impressed Sam so was that by the time he went and picked up the banker and the lady banker, and brought them back to the house and let them freshen up a little, and got over here to Dabney's drugstore in Rogers, they waited only a very few minutes until that son of Mr. Bradshaw was here from Marlin. He must have flown over those old rough roads. These roads were terrible out this way too at that time. I don't think it was paved, just graveled. The roads that were in the best condition back then were just gravel. They didn't start paving until years later.

The newspaper *The Daily Democrat* confirms some of Mrs. Dolehite's story regarding that night:

> They proceeded to a farm home and after information that they were safe had been conveyed to the Falls County sheriff's office by long distance telephone, they proceeded into Rogers where first details of the harrowing experience of the captives were related by Mr. Bradshaw.
> Scratches from some briars through which Miss Peyton

was forced to walk after being ordered out of the car in the pasture where they had spent the day was the only semblance of an injury.

What became of the loot obtained in robbery of the First State Bank of Marlin was a source of speculation for authorities. The Walker Gang was not seen placing the remainder of the money back in the car when they left the place. Officers were told that while the robbers' car was parked in a pasture near Rogers, the bandits removed the money from the automobile, extracting about five packages of $1 bills therefrom and some silver.

Report of a missing blanket from a Marlin tourist cottage where two men spent three nights preceding the bank robbery and kidnapping was connected by authorities with the fact that blankets were given to the captives by the bandits to keep them warm. The presence of the two men at the tourist park in a car answering the description of the one used in the robbery was being linked during the day of the robbery even before the captives were released. Whether the two robbers had one or more confederates as they claimed was still not known.

Meanwhile, authorities were entering the investigation with efforts to locate Walker and Thompson for questioning since they had received information that the men's photographs resembled the robbers. Deputy Sheriffs Hay and Stallworth went to Rogers, where Walker had been reared, and near where the captives were freed, in connection with the investigation. Officers had information that Walker was at Rogers about two weeks before the robbery at Marlin.

Falls County authorities investigating the First State Bank robbery were trying to pick up the two-day-old trail of a mud-spattered automobile reported at about 10:00 A.M. Friday at North Zulch. In a telephone message to the sheriff's office in Marlin, the constable at North Zulch reported the car, of the same make and model as that occupied by the two robbers seen in Marlin, occupied by two men fitting the descriptions of Walker and Thompson.

Fate is a strange thing. Sam Dolehite and his wife Violet were camping before Sam died in the late 1970s. Nobody had contacted Sam about the kidnapping after the night he piled all those cold and frightened people in his car back in December of 1933. Mrs. Dolehite tells a strange story:

My husband and I had a silver-streaked travel trailer. They were real good trailers, but not too many people had them in this part of the country. They were made in California. We were in Cloud Crow, New Mexico. We went up there for several summers. That would have been between 1970 and 1975.

Anyway, we were walking the loop around up there on the mountainside, and there was another silver streak trailer. This man was sitting out front of his trailer in a chair, like we do, you know, and we went by, and I said it out loud so that he could hear me, I said, "Oh, Sam. There's a man that knows a good trailer when he sees one." That just struck up a conversation with us, and we started talking and visiting.

When he said his name was Bradshaw, Sam asked him where he was from originally. One thing just led to another, and we found out that he was Mr. Bradshaw's son that had met Sam at Dabney's drug store to pick up his daddy. He and Sam were about the same age. Sam was about thirty years old when the robbery and kidnapping took place.

It was funny when they figured out who each other was. I don't remember who really figured out who was what, but Bradshaw stuck in Sam's mind, and Dolehite stuck in his. It really was funny.

So then we had many conversations as we walked back and forth and visited with each other. I think he and his wife were living in Phoenix, Arizona, at that time. We had a camp-fire nearly every night, and I think half the camp came down and sat around the campfire and we had more fun. That same summer the Bradshaws gave me a necklace and Sam a bolo tie.

During the robbery, Mr. Bradshaw had some silver dollars in his pocket. I think he had ten. He just had carried them in his pocket, and they didn't frisk him. The bank robbers did not frisk him, and the son still had those silver dollars. It was ten or twelve. I forgot what that young man told us. He wasn't young when he was talking to us. He said that he had them in his bank box, but he had just given most of them away. He said he wished he had more of them, and if he did, he would love to give Sam one. He only had about three left at that time. Sam said he wouldn't take one of them for anything. So then he made him the bolo tie and used one, but it wasn't one of those three.

The Whitey Walker Gang was gone. From an escape at the fishing hole in Oklahoma, these men had already successfully robbed a bank in Buckholts, a bank in Palestine, a jewelry store in Bryan, and a big haul in Marlin.

The Marlin robbery put these outlaws in a different league from the "Ma and Pa" drugstore bandits that plagued the Central United States. This robbery and kidnapping put the gang in the scope of a Dillinger, or a Pretty Boy Floyd. Not in style, or banner headlines perhaps, but in one calculated hit these escaped convicts were $41,000 richer. More importantly, they were still free. While half the Southwest law enforcement community were looking for the Bonnie and Clyde Gang, Whitey Walker, Mrs. Whitey Walker, Blackie Thompson, and Roy Johnson were smoking cigarettes and sipping whiskey on the road to Florida. They had a plan, and they had their targets.

Texas may have gotten a reprieve from the group's activities for a little while, but a V-8 automobile was heading toward the coast of Florida for some unsavory business. In the meantime, problems were brewing at a hell hole called Eastham State Prison in East Texas, and the people involved would start a chain of events that would overhaul the Texas penal system.

Chapter 7

Joe Palmer and Ray Hamilton Make Their Debut

J oseph Conger Palmer was born somewhere near Waco, Texas, on September 27, 1902, to Charles and Nora Palmer. He was born fourth of eight children, but that information would not be found in any prison records, nor would a list of his past employers. In a prison questionnaire that asked for information on employment, siblings, or contact person in case of death, Joe would put no one. Occasionally, he would acknowledge one sister out of necessity.[1] Bricks would not be thrown through his family's windows because of him. Whatever shame Joe may have brought to himself by his actions would not be passed on to his family, a family that included two Baptist preachers and a hardworking extended family that survived the lean years by following the oil booms of the 1920s.

Joe's occupation was a printer, a trade he became quite proficient at while serving time in various prisons. Many prisoners listed their occupation as farmer, but Joe was determined to learn something he could use as a skill wherever he went in life. Unfortunately, he would never need to apply his craft beyond prison walls.

His first brush with the law, like so many others during the time, involved auto theft. In Young County, Texas, he was arrested for auto theft in 1921. Sentenced on January 30, 1922, Palmer had his first taste of a Texas prison. He was eighteen

64

years old. A two-year sentence cost him fourteen months of his life as prisoner #47217. In 1924, less than a year after his discharge, the cell door closed on him again, this time in Oklahoma. While others started their lives of crime as chicken thieves, petty theft as teens, etc., Joe's excursions appeared to be systematic. Rumor had it that he would steal cars in Texas and have them refinished in Oklahoma, and then his contacts back in Texas would sell the vehicles. Whatever the situation was, on May 3, 1924, Joe Palmer entered the penitentiary at McAlester, Oklahoma, as prisoner #14236 with a five-year sentence for auto theft. This sentence from Tillman County lasted until June of 1927, when Palmer was discharged and he headed back to Texas.

Once he was back in his old stomping grounds of Central Texas, auto theft changed to burglary and general theft. He was particularly active in Navarro, Ellis, and Freestone counties, and he had developed quite an operation, however short-lived. He was caught again and given a string of two-year concurrent sentences back in Huntsville. On February 2, 1929, he was again released from prison and almost immediately escalated his criminal activity to armed robbery.[2] On May 6, 1929, Palmer, using the alias Joseph Jackson, walked into the Southern Pacific depot in Mexia, Texas, shortly after midnight.[3] With a single-action revolver, he told the agent to hand him the money from the safe. After retrieving around $300, the bandit ordered the agent outside to a waiting vehicle. As Palmer pointed the pistol at the company man, he forced the agent to drive him out of town. Two days later, while he rested in a tourist camp near Sherman, Texas, Palmer was captured by the Mexia police chief, A. R. Mace and John Piper, a special officer for the Southern Pacific.[4]

After Palmer plead guilty to robbery with firearms in Groesbeck, Texas, for the Mexia heist, something strange happened. The typed document that established sentencing instructions to the jury was altered by a handwritten change allowing the death sentence. Specifically, the instructions read:

GENTLEMEN OF THE JURY:
   The defendant, Joe Palmer, stands charged by indictment of the offense of robbery with firearms, alleged to have been committed in the County of Limestone and State of Texas on or about the 6th day of May, A.D. 1929. To this charge the

defendant had plead guilty, and has persisted in entering such a plea, notwithstanding the Court, as required by law, has admonished him of the consequences of the same; and it plainly appearing to the Court that the defendant is sane, and that he is not influenced to make said plea through any consideration of fear, nor by any persuasion or delusive hope of pardon prompting him to confess his guilt, said plea is by the Court received, and you are instructed to find defendant guilty as charged in the indictment, and to assess his punishment at death [added] or confinement in the State penitentiary by death or for any term of years, not less than five, as you may determine and state in your verdict.[5]

The jury chose to give Joe Palmer a twenty-five-year sentence in the Texas Prison System for his guilty plea of robbing Agent Lyles Justice of $300 at the depot. On May 20, 1929, he was back in the system as prisoner #61455.[6] He was sent to Central, one of the prison system's outlying farm units. He got along nicely during his nearly three years there, eventually working himself up to trustee job in one of the plow squads. In 1932 he was transferred to the Huntsville Unit. According to S. E. Barner, Print Shop Superintendent when Palmer was there, Joe became a first-class pressman.

Palmer was reported to keep to himself during his time at Huntsville. His only real interest was in the caged animals housed at the prison. Monkeys, coyotes, wolves, bears, and other species of wildlife were brought in by the management to help ease the monotony of prison life. To mistreat any of the animals was the one thing sure to earn the wrath of Joe Palmer.

An example was when one day another convict began jabbing the big brown bear with a pointed stick. Palmer, in a rage, challenged the animal baiter and a fight ensued. He was getting the better of his enemy when guards separated the two men. Palmer was sent to the Eastham Farm for punishment. From then on he would escape any time he saw an opportunity.[7]

At 2:30 A.M., a few weeks after his transfer to Eastham, trustee Palmer made his break. Going to work as a houseboy for an Eastham administrator, he seized the saddle horse belonging to the assistant farm manager and fled into the heavily wooded bottom land along the Trinity River. Riding until the horse gave out from exhaustion, he continued to flee on foot through the

East Texas river bottoms. By the time the escaped convict stopped to rest, his clothes had turned to shreds from the briar tangles and the scratches were beginning to fester. As the sun rose the next morning, he could make out the smoke from a chimney in the distance. The mud that had covered his prison clothes and the rips in the fabric gave him an idea. Approaching the farmhouse, he called for anyone there to come to the door.[8]

A farmer and his wife appeared at the door opening.

"I was taking my wife and baby to the doctor when my car broke down," Palmer told them, standing at a safe distance. "I need help. Can you lend me your car, neighbor?"

"My boy can drive you all to town," was the helpful response.

The farmer's fifteen-year-old son came out the front door and went to get the family's Ford pickup truck from the barn. The youth drove to where Palmer was on the road, and the mud-splattered convict got in the passenger seat. The teenager asked him where to go. Palmer pointed in the direction from where he had come, and stayed silent for three or four miles from the boy's home.

"Boy, I am an escaped convict. If you don't want to get hurt, jump out of here and skedaddle," Palmer told the farmer's son. He brought the automobile to a stop and then got out, staring at Palmer, and the escaped convict slid to the driver's side of the truck. The truck sped down the road toward the nearby town of Lovelady. Now that he had a vehicle, perhaps he had a chance.[9]

Turning onto the main asphalt road, he had about twenty miles to go before reaching the town. A bullet crashed into the truck. Then more shots came as Palmer could see two men with rifles following him about a quarter of a mile away in a black sedan. Another shot skimmed the top of his head, and the fugitive had had enough. He pulled to the side of the road.[10] One of the men who got out of the car behind the stolen truck was M. E. Gimon, a Special Texas Ranger living in Lovelady. The Ranger loaded the outlaw in the back of the car and returned him to Eastham. The lawman also collected his reward for capturing a fugitive.[11]

TEXAS PRISON SYSTEM
APPLICATION FOR WHIPPING

Farm or Prison Eastham Weldon, Texas
GENERAL MANAGER
HUNTSVILLE, TEXAS   September 19, 1933

Dear Sir:

I respectfully ask for an order from you to punish, by whipping, the following named convicts belonging to the force under my charge, to wit:

Register No.	Name	Violation of rules	No. of lashes
61466	Palmer Joe	Escaping while being	30
		trusted. Working as	
		Asst. Mgr. House	
		Boy and left farm	
		early AM on Capt.	
		Small's horse.	

I hereby certify that I have made full and careful inquiry in regard to the conduct of said convicts and especially in regard to the offenses charged, and am satisfied that the punishment asked for is deserved and is the only means that will bring the offender to terms. I have tried other means which have failed to produce the desired effects, as follows:

Here state means used: <u>This man's record clear except one minor offense in 1930.</u>

If such order is granted, same will be executed by me strictly in conformity with the requirements of said order and of the rules and regulations of the Prison System.

B. B. Monzingo   Manager   Warden

It would be another four months before Joe Palmer got another chance to escape from Eastham. The beatings he endured for not keeping up with the others in the field due to his spells of illness would not be forgotten. In mid-January, Joe would have his revenge.

RAYMOND HAMILTON

Volumes of information have been written on the notorious Raymond Hamilton, and it is not the intent of this book to re-hash what has already been written. A brief overview of his record is necessary, though, because anyone who can build sentences totaling over two and a half centuries in a four-year spree needs to be acknowledged. For further reading on this young man, see the footnote.[12]

Hamilton started out like so many others on the west side of Dallas. He got into trouble as a car thief, was more than willing to learn more, and got his wish by being good at what he did. Raymond would be the first to tell anyone how good he was at whatever he did. He was an escape artist and the best car thief ever seen by many of his criminal peers.

It was once said that giving another life sentence to Ray Hamilton was like pouring a bucket of water in Lake Dallas. He was a member of the Barrow Gang, but was so well known in his own right that sometimes the papers would refer to them as the Hamilton-Barrow Gang. He was not well liked by many people because he was a braggart and supposed stool pigeon. Whatever he was, or at least accused of being, he was a big thorn in the side of law enforcement. When he said that no prison could hold him, he was usually correct.

Raymond Elzie Hamilton was born on a Deep Fork river bank in a tent near Schulter, Oklahoma, to John and Alice Hamilton, May 21, 1913.[13] After his father worked different sawmill operations, he abandoned the family to the cares of a local prostitute in the winter of 1919. He had mortgaged the mill, taken all the money, and left the family without a word. They had contact with John over the years, but always with promises unkept and worse heartaches each time they trusted him. The last ruse took the Hamilton family to West Dallas, and that is where Raymond's story really begins.

The schools that Raymond, his older brother Floyd, and sisters Alice and Lillie attended were rough even by the standards of the west side, where lack of plumbing and electricity was the norm.[14] When John abandoned his family again he left them nothing but a car and a crisis regarding how to survive. Alice was through with her vagabond husband and divorced him. She married a chicken thief named Steve Davis in 1927, and they fought often.[15] Raymond had enough of all of it, and at fourteen he would never again return home on a regular basis. He did whatever he could to live, whether it was selling newspapers, stealing and selling bicycles, sleeping in alleys, or staying briefly with relatives.[16] It wouldn't be too long before Ray would be in the headlines of the same newspapers he hawked in the streets.

At five foot three-and-a-half inches, Ray weighed 121 pounds when he was introduced to the Texas Prison System. A person didn't have to be physically large to rob, but just needed a willingness to do it and a taste for continuing to do it. A twenty round-Browning Automatic Rifle didn't hurt matters much, either. The strangest twist is that Ray got his criminal start by selling stolen bicycles to the future sheriff of Dallas County, R.A. Smoot Schmid, when Schmid was a shop owner.[17] Everyone knew that Smoot had a "no questions asked" shop, and it would be Sheriff Schmid who years later would be directly involved in the quest to capture or kill Bonnie and Clyde. Raymond's earlier criminal career started with a car theft in September of 1931. He was caught and tried in the Second District Court in Dallas for auto theft and received a three-year sentence in the State Penitentiary. The sentence was suspended, however, and Ray walked away free. In only four months, he was sitting in a jail cell again, for grand theft auto in McKinney, Texas. This was where Ray left the world of small-time car theft to become a jail escapee, always on the run. Another prisoner on the outside and a friend of Bonnie and Clyde, Ralph Fults, smuggled him hacksaw blades to cut the bars for his escape.[18] Hamilton moved up the criminal ladder quickly by robbery with a firearm and burglary.[19]

What finally got Ray a life sentence was a robbery and murder that he didn't actually commit. On April 30, 1932, Ray Hamilton was nowhere near Hillsboro when Clyde Barrow and two companions banged on the door of J. N. and Martha

Bucher, owners of a combination gas station, general merchandise, and jewelry store located on the old Fort Worth Highway. Using the ploy that one of the bandits needed a guitar string in the middle of the night, the sixty-five-year-old owner was persuaded to come down from his bedroom located on the second floor and let the men into the building.[20] Some reports stated that Clyde was in the getaway car and not in the building at all.[21] One of the bandits gave Bucher a ten dollar bill for a twenty-five-cent string, knowing that he would have to open the safe to get change. That's when trouble really started.

J. N. called to his wife to come down with the safe combination. She did, and after she gave the thief his change she turned to close the safe, but they had different plans. A .45 caliber pistol appeared in the hands of one of the badmen, and the jeweler went for a pistol of his own.[22] A crack of flame in the near darkness, the explosion of a pistol's discharge, and the old man was dying with a bullet in his chest. His wife surprised the gunman when she went for her husband's gun then, but she was quickly subdued by the gunmen. Their take from the safe was forty dollars in cash and about fifteen hundred dollars' worth of jewelry. Now murder was involved, and if there was any turning back for Clyde Barrow, it was now gone. He didn't know that his friend Ray was soon to take the fall and receive a life sentence for that robbery and murder.

Ray was involved in a series of holdups with the Barrow Gang after the Hillsboro affair. He proved to have many accomplices, and no place in the midwestern United States seemed safe from him. Packing houses, banks, nothing was off limits, and no stickup was too dangerous. Raymond was wanted for robbery and murder in Oklahoma, kidnapping with the Barrow Gang in New Mexico, bank robberies throughout Texas, jail escape in Texas, and for scaring the hell out of the general public.[23] Hamilton's name promoted fear, and like the Barrow Gang, every robbery anywhere in the Midwest could be blamed on him. Raymond was not invincible, however, and after his split with Bonnie and Clyde, he and a partner name Gene O'Dare went to Bay City, Michigan, to live it up for awhile, since things in Texas were a little too hot.

Unfortunately for Ray, he sometimes let his hormones do

his thinking for him. After he and O'Dare got to Bay City, they went to an ice skating rink where they were supposed to meet two women.[24] What they found instead was the wrong end of pistols drawn by the Michigan State Police. They were completely unable to do anything defensive with ice skates on, although O'Dare tried to pull a .38 caliber pistol and was knocked down by one of the policeman. Raymond knew it was futile to resist and let the arrest take its course.[25] The two were arrested on December 6, 1932, and by December 14 it was back to Dallas. It was time for one of Texas' most dangerous men to go back home.

Hamilton was wanted badly by both Oklahoma and Texas, but after a jailbreak attempt in Dallas and other exploits, it was the Hillsboro trial that he feared most. Martha Bucher at first said she didn't recognize Hamilton as the gunman, but after extreme pressure from law enforcement she consented to mark him as the killer.[26] On March 18, 1933, Ray received life behind bars. He was spared electrocution, due in part to his boyish looks. On August 8, 1933, Ray was in the back of Bud Russell's one-way wagon with a chain around his neck.[27] Raymond Hamilton was sentenced to pick cotton for 263 years at Eastham State Farm.

CHAPTER 8

Rabbit Runs at Eastham

Everything. I've done everything on the farm. Some of it. Little of it. Wasn't very good at none of it." These are the words of Troy Knighten, a man with a thirty-year pin at the Texas Prison System. From 1950 to 1980, Troy worked at Eastham Farm, one of the original penal facilities, which is located near Weldon, Texas. He was also in charge of the dog packs that were used to chase down escaped convicts. As he sat in a chair, a person could visualize him on a horse many years ago, maybe with sunglasses on, dogs barking in front as he chased someone through the thicket while they tried to get to the Trinity River before the dogs got to them first. Troy started his career at Old Eastham, the dormitory prison that is now a gutted building, the same building that housed Clyde Barrow, Joe Palmer, Ray Hamilton, and many others during the years of the Great Depression. Troy continued:

> They used to raise cotton, corn, maize. Had a big garden. They don't even have a garden down there no more. They had more cotton than anything else. Well, they had a lot of peas, stuffed corn, maize, but cotton, they had the cotton hand picked. They had a gin there. I guess the old gin is still standing.
>
> The line squad turned out about seven o'clock in the morning. Come in about six that evening. Something like that.

According to what they are doing. If they were picking cotton, it'd be dark before they got in. They didn't go out if there was a big rain.

You would think they wouldn't want to come back to prison after working those fields the first time, but a lot of them did. I had one of those boys tell me one time, he said he was going home. He said, "I'll see you in about three months." I was up there at the dog house one day, and I looked down the road, and I seen that son-of-a-bitch coming. I told another dog boy, come here and look. We called him Wino. He was an old, tall, slender man. I said, "Here comes old Wino." He had stayed out three months.

If a convict messed up, he was off to solitary on the side of the building. He wouldn't stay in too long, though. As for meat on the farm, they had their own butcher back then. Later on they got to sending it to a packing plant down there on the Central Farm. Then they started trucking it, bringing it to the farm. I don't know if they still have that plant open or not. There was also a big dairy at Eastham.

Every now and then, one of the convicts would try and run for it. Well, everybody that was working would have to go in for a lockdown. Just as quick as they'd find he's gone, we would let the dogs loose and try to pick up the trail. Wherever they run off from, that's where you want to go start dragging your dogs and pick his track up, following by horse. I've gone a many a mile through those woods on horseback trying to stay up with them dogs. You gotta' stay up with them dogs. Don't you lose 'em.

There was red bone, blue tick, black, and tan dogs. They were mixed up, and ran about eight dogs in a pack. For a long time I had four packs. Called 'em One Pack, Two Pack, Three Pack, Four Pack.

They had pens or houses for them not too far from the old cotton gin. Had a dog house, a little old house, and we had our pens back there. And some time, there weren't more than three or four dogs to a pen. We carried a pack to the field every day, out where the line was working. A pack of dogs, with a dog boy to take the pack to the field. Well, he'd sit on the ground watching everything.

When a convict ran off, whichever way he was going, they'd load up some of them guard bosses and space them out. It would be just like putting them on a deer stand. That's the way it was done. Well, sometimes a convict would get treed, and sometimes they'd beat the dogs. Most of the time, lots of times, they'd catch them on the ground. If it's night or something like that, most of them would go up a tree. If they caught them on the ground, well—they'd catch 'em. Then we would call the dogs off when we got there.

They'd surprise you, too. Those convicts could go a long ways sometimes. Most of them would go to the Trinity River. They'd think they'd beat those dogs, and they did. Sometimes they did. They'd get in the river. Well, lots of times those damn convicts would go down and stay in that water. Go way on down the river and then get out.

There wasn't any fans or anything for the heat in that old building. They had heaters in there in the winter time, wood heaters. They cooked with wood. Had those big wood cookstoves. We had to go to the woods to cut wood. That's what we did in the winter time, cut wood.

The trustees stayed upstairs, and the linemen stayed downstairs. There was a laundry shack down there and it had the big old pots to boil them clothes in. They had clotheslines made out of barbed wire. Yeah, it was on the outside way down there by the blacksmith's shop. They'd just take 'em and throw up over the barbed wire they had stretched up there, that clothesline. Didn't have to have clothes pins or nothing.

Those convicts used to be bad about cutting their heel string. That was back, 40s early 50s, when many of them did that. A lot of them done it. But, later on, I never known of one cutting their heel strings. Sometimes they'd send them off and sometimes they'd just keep them at a kind of little old hospital there. They had a dentist and all that kind of stuff.

They closed off Old Eastham in 1958 when they got that new building built. They moved them right on over there just as quick as they got it. Well, they didn't have it fixed when they moved them over there. They just had part of it finished.

You know one time, before they built all those houses, I was running the tracking dogs. I came across where now it's all done cleared out, and a dog boy was with me, and we was coming across there on horseback. My horse hit something like a piece of iron or something, and kicked it up. It was a damned old pistol. Yeah, it wasn't nothing but the barrel, and uh, wood stock handles, you know those wooden handles, it was gone and the cylinder was gone. Just a barrel and the handle.

I gave it to Warden Rush and he was supposed to put it in some kind of museum or something. He told me that he had

somebody test it and it was a .32 pistol. Instead of a .38, he had
a .32. In other words, it wasn't no state gun. See the state used
.38s and 30-30s. And, the Warden told me that was a .32. It
had been on the ground a long time.

Another guard wishing to remain anonymous tells a story of
how one convict years ago was chased by the dog packs until he
couldn't run anymore, and so he climbed a tree.

> They let the packs go after a runaway near dark. It wasn't
> long before they had him up a tree. Well the dogs just bark at
> the base of that big tree because they can't get to this guy.
> When the Boss rode up on his horse he told that convict to
> jump down out of that tree. That convict said there was no way
> he was jumping down into all those dogs. That Boss pulled out
> his hogleg pistol and shot at the base of that tree. Then he put
> one a little farther up, and farther still, until the next round
> was pointed at that runaway. The boss says, "Boy, do we have
> a dead runaway or are you going to jump out of that damn
> tree?" He jumped out of the tree and started screaming when
> those dogs went into him. The dog boys called the hounds off
> right away. They marched that convict back to the 'ham and
> threw him in solitary for a few days.

Everyone understood the unwritten rules of escape at Eastham. Generally, an escaped convict heads towards the river. The
convict knows it, the guards on horseback know it, and when the
dog pens open the dogs know it because they have been there.
Occasionally a convict working the fields will cut off his toes with
the slip of an axe, or an aggie hoe gone wild. Sometimes others
do it for them for a price. Sometimes there's a slip and the heel
string is sliced so that a field convict can no longer work the
sunup to sundown agony of the cotton lines or the wood details.
Something about the howling and the baying of the hounds
tells the whole atmospheric story about Old Eastham. It somehow describes everything. A convict decides the best time, maybe in the morning before it gets too hot. Maybe later when the
guards are bored, leaning over in their saddles hoping the highrider hiding in the woods won't see them off in the distance.
Maybe at that point when he throws his aggie hoe down, maybe
that's when he runs for the woods or the fields when the growth

is tall, that's when he bolts for the river. The Trinity. The Trinity is what many of these men are hoping is the ticket to freedom. Maybe if he gets in the river and goes down long enough, he'll get away before they can find him. Maybe he can get there before the dogs do.

When a convict bolts he really does not want to be caught. Bleeding when he comes back down out of the tree, or after the dogs have tasted him some so the others know what happened when you run. That is referred to as "Not disappointing the dogs."

Some of the prison farms used to treat a discipline problem prisoner to solitary confinement. He would be stripped down naked with nothing in there but a steel bunk and a hole in the ground. That's why it's called the Shitter. A person who has been in there a few days loses track of the time. It's so dark you can't see your hand in front of your face, you don't know if it's day or night outside, don't know what day it is. Those kind have to be released at night because of their eyes. In the field if the mosquitos don't tear you up, it's the chigger bugs or the ticks or the sweltering heat.

It's not always the convicts you have to worry about. Sometimes it's your fellow guards. Take for example this one boy who would drive to work and when he got there he parked his car real close to a big tree. Then he'd pull out a chain and he'd wrap this chain all in and out through the bumper and padlock it to the tree so that nobody would steal it. He was really more paranoid than that. For example, when it was chow time, all the inmates would go in for lunch. This guy, he would stand apart from them. He would never accept a tray of food from an inmate. He always figured they were out to poison him, so he would just sit back on his own for a while watching as the convicts got their trays of food one by one down the line, and then at some imaginary moment that only he could understand, he would jump up and run over to one of the prisoners, grab the tray of food from their hands, and take it back over to his seat. That way he knew it was safe. Surely they wouldn't poison one of their own.

That's not the strangest part with this guy. There would be the days, he would be on horseback. I won't give a name, don't know if I could remember it even if I tried. See this guy

was actually in charge of a squad of men, and when the prisoners would go out to the fields chopping cotton, gathering
wood, whatever, depending on the season, then . . .

This guy, he'd get them out there in that field, and you
wouldn't believe this, but what this guy would do is watch those
men work; and he would undo his pants, and he'd just place
his testicles right out there on top of that saddle. Then he'd
pull out that frog sticker knife he'd always carry with him, and
as those men chopped the weeds between the cotton rows this
guy would slide that knife back and forth across his testicles,
pulling off any chiggers or gnats or bugs that were on him. All
morning long, he'd just slowly scrape his testicles with that
frog sticker and he'd watch those men as they chopped cotton.
Trust me, if one of those men got too slow, wouldn't keep up
with that hoe line, he'd call them over there. Everybody knew
that something was going to happen. They would come over
and say, "Yes, Boss man?" He'd say, "Boy, pick up that stick,"
pointing down at the ground at something laying near by.
Well, as this convict leaned over to pick up the stick, this guard
would pull out his service revolver and shoot near the convict's
head. Of course the convict jumps, not knowing what was
going on. Well, then this guy would sit there for about five
minutes screaming at the top of his lungs at this man, asking
him why he jumped and what did he think he was doing staying behind the rest of that line. Asking him why he's so lazy.
Anyway, just another story. Thought you'd want to know.

Pete Wells, who like Troy Knighten spent a career at Eastham prison, worked in the postal area. Pete gave a different per-
spective of the place. He shared the story of Jack the Turnkey:

Take for example old Jack the Turnkey. A Turnkey was a
building tender, a convict in control of door keys. For some
reason, Jack always had a claw hammer. He used it to keep the
other convicts in check. You'd take that claw hammer away
from him, and it wouldn't be ten minutes he'd have another.
Lord knows where he got them from, I just didn't know, but
Jack wouldn't go anywhere without a claw hammer. I remember Eastham. I remember all kinds of stories. I remember that
machine shop near the window. The machine shop window
over there near the dorm is where they would slip weapons
through. They'd bust those windows all the time to get down
to there. Get down to that shop. You take a solitary confine-

ment at Eastham and you're looking at about a four-by-eight metal door. I'm talking about a closed metal door. You didn't even know what day it was after you got in there for a little while. Leave them crammed together all night for not picking cotton. They caught on. They'd be picking cotton the next day, that's for sure.

Like that old boy from Mississippi. I don't remember exactly where, but that was a farm that he came from. When he'd take his shirt off you could see those Mississippi beatings from where he was at. You could see scars from that big old back strap from one end of his back to the other. Yeah, it was different back then, prisoners—convicts we called them—cut their heelstrings to get out of work. Some of those boys would steal liquid shoe polish. They'd also steal that mithiolate. Guess they got it from the prison hospital. They'd drip it in a bowl with cotton balls and drink it.

You want to talk about dogs, I remember the dogs and I also remember a guy making a run for it. Yeah, he made a run for it, all right, he was running for that river. He thought he'd be real smart. He was going to outsmart everybody. He thought what he had was a shortcut through a culvert. Culvert, like a big long drainage ditch. He got down in that big old long culvert. Those dog boys let go of those dogs and you got one pack running behind him. He didn't know it, but another pack went on around to the other end of that culvert. About the time he hit the middle, you got four dogs coming up one side, you got four coming from the other. That culvert was long, and the only way to get those dogs off was when the dog boys get down in there, they call them off. But if you don't hear those dog boys, they don't stop. The dog boys yelled, but those dogs couldn't hear the commands to stop. They just keep on doing what they were trained to do . . .

Hugh Kennedy lit the stub of a cigar he had in the ashtray and leaned back in his chair. He was one of the few still living that "swung that aggie hoe" through the early 1930s Eastham years. He turned off the police scanner that he usually keeps on the way people keep radios on, just to have some noise in the background.

"That boss had no reason to shoot that boy," Kennedy said after figuring out the right way to start the story:

I was with the plow squad then. They moved me to the Retrieve Farm. I had a money operation going on at the Walls, twenty-five cents on the dollar. There was a big gambling operation going on and people would need money to stay in the game. Cards, dice, whatever. Special favors cost twenty dollars. That's just the way it worked. Anyway, after I couldn't run from the dogs no more I got caught and ended up at Retrieve. I had escaped from the Meridian jail and worried about those dogs for months. You never forget that barking when those dogs get close to you on the trail. I slept in sheep pens, rubbed wild mint on my face and hands, stuffed it in my pockets to get those dogs confused. One time I had to jump off an embankment into some trees so those dogs would have to go way around to get down to me. Finally those dogs got close again. I punctured my leg twice, real close together, then stumbled to the front of a farmhouse yelling I'd been snake bit and needed a doctor. Back then I was using the name Robert Merideth. These people loaded me in a car to take me to the closest town. I was going to jump out of the car as soon as we put some miles between me and those dogs. The car came around a sharp bend in the road and half the county laws had us roadblocked. Well, that was the end of that, and I ended up at Retrieve. That was in 1938 or 1939, I think. That was a few years after I had been at the Eastham Farm. That was the only good thing I ever learned from Eastham, how to blindside those dogs.

Anyway, we were working the fields one day and this boy, a convict working with us, had to go relieve himself. Now all those bosses, the guards, they were on horses. They had shotguns, mostly. This boy stops working and goes to the fence to take a piss. I guess he wanted some privacy, I don't know, but he goes over the fence and undoes his pants. That Boss drew a bead on that boy and shot him in the stomach. I ran over to that boy. He was screaming and trying to hold his guts. His pants were falling down, and while he was holding his guts I refastened his pants. That Boss just stared at us. It wasn't much longer that the boy died. Back then nothing was much said, because you couldn't do anything about it anyway.[1]

One time that same bastard guard got mad at somebody in the squad. Everybody was kind of grouped together in the field. This Boss didn't say nothing, didn't warn anybody. He levels that gun and starts letting it fly. Shoots right into everybody. That bastard killed three men and never even said why he was mad.[2] I had decided long before that I was going to sneak a camera in and take some pictures. That's what I did, too. I had one of those small cameras you could palm in your hand. I would be in the field and have that camera in my hand. I could spread my fingers out and take a picture so it wouldn't be so obvious. When the film was out I would bribe a guard to have it developed and then he would bring it back to me. A lot of them knew I had it but didn't say anything. I wasn't supposed to have it, but I pretty much got along with the laws and I could come and go as I pleased. When I got shipped over the Central Farm, now Sugarland, they let me take my pictures. I started the first school at Central. You would be surprised how many of the people couldn't even sign their own name. I told the captain that if he gave twenty days overtime to these men I would find the students. The captain finally agreed, and the next day fifty or so had signed up. We started school that same night. Something else you always hear about, how we grew our own food and all that. We were sick, all of us. That food didn't come our way. A convict would sometimes not eat for three or four days because we ate stew that was maggot-infested. That was our farm-bred meal. Sometimes men would go out of the fields with a boss and not come back. Things were bad, real bad. I worked in the packing house before I taught school. We would make these big sausages. Sometimes I would find some fresh bread and cut off a piece of one of those sausages. I can still taste it.

Then there was the "ring" for punishment. Sunup to sundown a man was tied down in only his underwear in a pit. It wasn't the fact that he was tied down, it was that he was tied over a bed of red ants, the more you moved the more they stung; sometimes they went for your eyes . . .

CHAPTER 9

Welcome to the 'ham:
Prelude to a Raid

I f there was ever a poster boy for someone who should stay in the penitentiary, it would be James Mullins. He was born to Irish immigrants in Williamsport, Pennsylvania, on September 26, 1885. Mullins was classified as incorrigible at an early age. His criminal record began on November 7, 1905, for larceny, using the alias James F. Kinley.

For this crime Mullins served fourteen months in jail and was then paroled from Philadelphia. From 1909 through 1912 he was incarcerated in the Pennsylvania Industrial School. He was received, paroled, and returned as a violator. His record early on consisted of poor conduct with at least thirteen months of general crookedness, disobedience of orders, and fighting.

As though he was bored with his regular lawbreaking, while under his alias James F. Kinley, he broke into a railroad car, which both violated his parole and cost him thirteen months in jail. Mullins seemed to stay on track for awhile after his August 31, 1915, discharge, but in December 1920 he was back at it again under the alias James Miller in Atlanta and Cleveland. His violation of the Interstate Commerce Act cost him an eighteen-month stretch. By March 1923 Mullins, still alias James Miller, started what would prove to be a lifelong obsession with narcotics. He was charged with violating the drug act and sentenced in Cleveland for one year and a day. He stayed in an Ohio jail from March 28, 1923, until his discharge on January 6, 1934. By October of that year, Mullins was sent to Levenworth Penitentiary in Kansas on drug violations for two years, and he was not released until October 9, 1926. Until Levenworth he was just a dope fiend with a bad habit of getting caught. At Levenworth Mullins led an unsuccessful mutiny in the dining hall. As soon as he was discharged from the Kansas prison, he got mixed up in breaking and entering, which earned him a five- to fifteen-year sentence in February 1927 using the alias James Muller.

This time he would not be paroled until April of 1931. It only took two months for Mullins, now going by the alias James Lamont, to be arrested by Houston police for an attempted burglary. Apparently he was released, because in August of 1931 San Antonio police arrested him for a burglary, and this time the charge would stick. Mullins headed to Huntsville for a three-year sentence. From the Walls Unit, Mullins was going to the punishment farm at Eastham as convict #69041, and he would stay there until January 10, 1924.

In March of 1932 he received twelve lashes with regulation strap for refusing to work. It was during this sentence at Eastham that Mullins became acquainted with Raymond Hamilton. According to Mullins' own admission later, Hamilton went to him with a proposition because he was known to have a very long criminal record and was respected for his knowledge of penitentiaries and for having numerous contacts on the outside.

Hamilton approached Mullins about a possible prison break. After considerable discussion, Mullins agreed to contact Hamilton's brother Floyd after he was discharged from the Texas Prison System and to arrange to smuggle guns to Hamilton so that Hamilton might use the guns to effect an escape from the Eastham State Farm. He didn't want Joe Palmer in on the deal, however. Mullins believed that Palmer was stir-simple and that it was dangerous to have such a man in on this kind of escape or the criminal activity that was likely to follow.[1]

HILTON BYBEE

Whereas James Mullins had the traits of a "what's in it for me" at anyone's expense kind of person, Hilton Bybee was just flat-out ruthless. Born June 10, 1910, to Omer and Bula Bybee, Hilton's family lived at Baileyboro, Texas. Hilton considered himself a farmer by occupation, and he had served in the Twelfth Calvary Troop E, beginning in 1927. It was his position as a soldier at Fort Sam Houston, in fact, that really started his trouble. On May 18, 1931, Bybee was confined to the post prison with a charge of the 58th Article of War. This may have been related to a San Antonio spree in February 1931, when Bybee was arrested for robbery, felonious assault, and auto theft. No result of either arrest is given. In the San Antonio spree, Bybee used the alias William Floyd Stewart, and that's how his name is entered as #6667.[2]

By February of 1932 however, Bybee was near his hometown in Cottle County, Texas. Hilton, also known as W. H., and his brother Otis had plans for February 28, 1932. Ernest Slape was minding his own business at his friend Skeet Hood's house in Paducah, Texas, that Sunday afternoon. A. V. Davidson, Skeet Hood's wife, and three or four others were there. So was a man unknown to Ernest, a man he would learn later to be named Hilton Bybee. Slape didn't stay long, maybe ten or fifteen minutes. Bybee was still there when Slape decided around five or six o'clock that evening it was time to go home.[3]

It was between nine and ten o'clock that night when Slape's life turned into a nightmare. The gathering at Skeet Hood's shifted to Slape's house in town, not by design but by circumstance. Mrs. Anna Renfro and her husband, Buck, had gone to the house with Skeet's wife, Maud, and Mrs. Curly Fullingim. Mrs. Hood had a sick child and wanted to see if they could borrow Slape's car. When they had arrived, Ernest and one of the Davidson boys were there.[4]

Maud Hood would remember later that she had seen the Bybee brothers taking three pistols they had hidden under a pillow at Skeet's house earlier that evening right before they had left the house. It made her nervous at the time, and maybe she should have said something after the two had left the house.[5] She went out on the porch with Mrs. Fullingim because they were fixing to leave. The women walked out on the porch and stood by a tree just as the Bybee brothers came on the porch. Hilton had two pistols in his hands, his brother Otis had one.[6]

Otis looked at the people standing on the porch and told them, "Get in the house."[7] Ernest happened to be sitting next to the front door. Hilton went through the door with a gun in each hand. "You are the guy we want, get out of here," Hilton told Slape.

There was no hesitation when the gunman went up close to Ernest and said, "You get out of here, or I'll knock you in the head with one of these guns."[8]

Otis was standing outside the door. When Ernest stepped out of the house he started to run four or five steps toward the direction of town. Hilton Bybee raised his pistol and fired. He shot the running man between the shoulders. As the bullet penetrated his back, Ernest fell to the ground. The brothers walked to the fallen man and got the money out of his pockets as he lay there bleeding. They both pilfered his pockets, Hilton taking the money out of the left pocket, and Otis out of the right. Loud enough for everyone to hear, Hilton then told his brother, "They don't go far when this hits them," referring to his pistol.[9]

The total haul netted by the brothers was $104; a fifty dollar bill, a twenty, one ten dollar bill, three fives, and some ones.[10] The thieves then ran toward a car in the distance, leaving the man on the ground in front of his friends and neighbors with a bullet that had entered his back between the shoulders and lodged in his neck. Since the house and porch lights were on during the entire robbery, the identities of the Bybees were clearly visible.[11] The man on the ground had most of his money in one pocket, creating a bulge, when he was at the Renfro's place earlier in the day. It is assumed that the brothers noticed the bulge while at the gathering.[12]

There was a road that led from an old highway to the house. This old road, the Qunnah Road, went east and then turned as it crossed a canyon. The road led north towards the highway, just as it reached the top of a hill. The house was set back from the street a little way.[13] A car was sitting about two blocks north of the house. Anna could see it, because she and A. V. Davidson slipped out the back door after they heard the gunshot. She also saw two men run toward that car. As they drove off, she saw the tail lights of the car as it started to speed off near a neighbor's fence toward some Gulf tanks heading north or northwest.[14] Anna had only been at Slape's about three minutes before the shooting.[15]

Hilton Bybee was arrested at a house by Young County Sheriff J. B. Foster on March 17 and turned over to the custody of a Sheriff Morrow of Stephens County. Found in the house when Bybee was arrested were two of the guns he had at the Slape shooting, a .45 and a .38 caliber pistol.

On April 27, 1932, Hilton Bybee, alias Shelton Bybee, had his day in court. The result was inevitable after the overwhelming evidence against him:

> It is the order of the court that the defendant, Hilton Bybee, who has been adjudged to be guilty of the offense of robbery with firearms, and whose punishment has been assessed by the verdict at death, shall on the 20 days of January, A.D., 1933, the state penitentiary of Huntsville, Walker County, Texas, be electrocuted at any time before sunrise on said date, by causing to pass through the body of said Hilton Bybee, a current of electricity of sufficient intensity to cause death and the application of the continuance of such current through the body of the said Hilton Bybee until he is dead.[16]

That was not all for Bybee, now Texas prisoner #72292. He also had a murder charge waiting for him in Stephens County, as well as a robbery with firearms. The murder charge gave him a life sentence, and a robbery at Throckmorton an additional twenty-five-year sentence in Texas penitentiaries. Although his appeals were fruitless, Bybee did receive several stays of execution. The end result was a commutation of sentence by the governor to a life term to run concurrently with his life sentence for the Stephens County murder. He would now go back to prison as W. H. Bybee, #72718. He was finally home at the Eastham State Farm.[17]

J. B. FRENCH

J. B. French was a juvenile delinquent who just didn't know when to quit. He was born on August 4, 1909, to John and Annie French in McAlester, Oklahoma. He was the third of four children, his only sister dying near the time of his birth.

His father was a railroad engineer and fireman, and the family frequently moved from one railroad town to another, first to Atoka, Oklahoma, and then to Oklahoma City. In 1923 the family moved to Denison, Texas, where their nomadic progress stopped. This was home. J. B. attended public schools at Atoka, Oklahoma City, and Denison, going as far as the seventh grade of public schools in Denison in 1925.

In 1922 he started committing burglaries in Grayson County, Texas. Soon he left Grayson County, and at Pecos, Texas, he stole a car. After being apprehended in New Mexico, French was returned to Pecos, where he was tried and sentenced to six months in the reformatory at Gatesville.

However, on the way to Gatesville he escaped and fled back to Grayson County. Already on the run, French committed a series of robberies. In the northern part of the county he had a hideout and was finally arrested with a cohort named Sam Forrest. The result was a six-year sentence in the Texas Prison System for burglary and robbery charges.

Entering prison in February of 1927, French immediately became a discipline problem. During 1927 he was punished on four different occasions; twice for laziness, once for staying in a building without permission, and once for cutting up cotton. The fourth punishment resulted in his being whipped. Again, a few months later, he was punished for lying in the building without permission.[18]

On June 3, 1929, he was granted a ninety-day furlough by Texas Governor Moody. This was extended to sixty more days on July 5, 1929. For whatever reason, French just could not keep himself clear of criminal activity. While out on furlough, he decided to steal an automobile in Lawton, Oklahoma. He was apprehended at Muskogee, Oklahoma, where he was charged with automobile theft. He was tried and sentenced to five years in the reformatory at Granite, given the prison number 7313.[19]

After being in the Granite reformatory for awhile, French decided to escalate his activities to full-scale mutiny. September 21, 1931, would be the day for a planned escape. Leading twenty-three others, French and his band had two guns smuggled into the prison. They overpowered the guards that night and forced the night warden to call the front picket away from their posts. The mob of escapees then stole the cars that belonged to the guards and drove to freedom. French left on his own without any of the other escaped prisoners. According to Texas prison records, French later named some of the other individuals involved in the escape:

> Leon Lemons—co-leader; Clarence Hays—who was later killed at Sapuopa, Oklahoma; Finis Beer—who was later killed resisting officers at Ardmore, Oklahoma; Charles Snider; Jack Bernard; John Henderson; Donald Bean; Doyle Bean; Frank Silas; and Howard Quarter [French thought that Quarter later died in the electric chair at McAlester for having killed a fellow inmate].[20]

While out on this escape, it was necessary for French to frequently change cars, and in doing so it was necessary for him to hold up the owners of the cars and take their automobiles away from them. He committed such offenses in Fannin, Grayson, and Hunt Counties in Texas. In connection with these offenses he would be charged with robbery by assault with firearms.

The first of these offenses occurred in Fannin County and when he was apprehended and taken to Fannin County for trial, he attempted to escape from the Fannin County jail. In making this attempt he assaulted the jailer, and for that offense he was also charged with assault to murder. He was then transferred to jail in Lamar County, where there was a robbery charge against him. While in jail there, he affected an escape with Floyd Basham and Johnny Reno. French, Basham, and Reno stole automobiles from Hunt County and Grayson County. They were finally arrested while staying at a farm house near Pottsboro in Grayson County, Texas.

French was then tried in Grayson and Hunt Counties and sent to the penitentiary. After he arrived at the penitentiary, he wrote the sheriff of Robertson County that he had committed the robbery of a grocery store in that county. The strange part of that is he did not commit the robbery, but he wanted to be taken to the Robertson County jail in order to attempt an escape. However, he was not able to escape, was tried on the robbery charge he instigated himself, and was sentenced to five years and returned to the penitentiary.[21] Given sentences for robbery with firearms, attempted murder, kidnapping, and auto theft, French had lost any hope of leniency from law enforcement. It was time for this troublemaker to pay.

French was headed for the wood crew at the Burning 'ham.

CHAPTER 10

"He Didn't Give Me a Dog's Chance"

H ugh Kennedy woke early in his bunk at the dormitory of Old Eastham. He thought back to the first night he had arrived for getting in trouble again after Governor Miriam "Ma" Ferguson had granted him a furlough when she visited the farm. Every time he tried to get stable work, the cops would hassle him for anything that happened in the county and he would get run off the job. Finally he decided to give them something to hassle him for, and now he was back in Eastham as a parole offender for an armed robbery. That's where they sent the convicts they wanted to teach a lesson, particularly the area known as South Eastham. *This is a murder house*, Kennedy thought to himself.[1]

The building tender said they didn't have a mattress available for him, but he pointed to a bunk on the lowest of the three level bed racks. "You can use that one tonight. That guy's in the hospital. We'll get you your own mattress tomorrow." Hugh looked down at the mattress; it looked like two sheets sewn together it was so thin. Kennedy, alias Robert Meredith, was tired, so he went on to sleep.[2]

It was after midnight when he woke that night. Something was tapping on his face. It was pretty dark in the unit, and he wiped the side of his face. Something sticky was all over the side of his face and neck. The new prisoner leaned up on his elbow

90

in his bunk and put his hand nearer his face so he could see it. It was blood, and another drop landed on him as he looked up at the mattress above him. The bottom of the second-tier bed was saturated in one spot, and blood seeped through it, landing on him. "Building tender," Kennedy hissed in the silence across the room.

Someone stirred nearby. A convict got up from his bunk and started walking toward Hugh's bunk. Kennedy stood up from his bunk and the two saw a dead man lying in a pool of blood, so lacerated with cuts it was hard to make out his features. "He's dead. Go back to sleep, we can't do nothing about it now," the other convict told him. Not knowing what else to do, Kennedy switched ends of his mattress and went back to bed.

That was then. It was time for the field squads to wake up and get ready for work. They had stacked wood until dark the day before, and they were going back again this morning. Plow Squad One was where Hugh was the lead man. His friend Joe Palmer was in the squad with him, as well as Raymond Hamilton, Hilton Bybee, Henry Methvin, and several other men. The lead man wondered what Hamilton meant when he asked him the previous day, "Do you like Hillsboro? I'm going there tomorrow." *Smart aleck,* Hugh thought. *Always popping off about something, that's why nobody likes him.*[3]

The running joke regarding Texas weather changing at any given time was true again on January 16, 1934. It could have just as easily been a blue norther across the sky, but instead the temperature that morning would be in the fifties, climbing to the sixties mark during the day.[4]

Earlier in the month, James Mullins had been discharged from Eastham Prison. After his January 10 release, Mullins wasted no time lighting out for West Dallas in search of Raymond Hamilton's brother, Floyd. Raymond and Mullins had already discussed in detail the arrangements for a prison break. Raymond had told Mullins to bring guns down to the Eastham Farm and meet him with a car.[5] Several different arrangements had been made, but the understanding was that when Mullins came down to Eastham he was to get Hilton Bybee and Raymond Hamilton. Joe Palmer was also to be included, and over Mullins' objection.[6]

When the final plan was set on January 10, Mullins was to come to Eastham and bring some guns in a car. When he was discharged, he went to see Floyd Hamilton in West Dallas. First he went to see Raymond's sister, but there was a man there at the house and Mullins didn't want to discuss business in front of him. Mullins saw Floyd Hamilton the next night, and told him of the arrangements that had been made. It was soon after that the two went and met Clyde Barrow and Bonnie Parker.[7]

After that they came back to Dallas and stayed the night at Floyd's house. Initially, they were supposed to carry the guns down to the Eastham Farm the following Sunday. The guns were to be placed under a bridge, about 150 to 200 yards from the main building on the farm. The guns were supposed to be carried into the building by a trustee. After spending the night with Floyd, Mullins went downtown and bought a box of cartridges and two or three clips for two .45 army pistols. Clyde Barrow furnished one of the pistols, and Floyd had one at his house. When they got the pistols and the ammunition, they went down to Eastham on the Saturday before the date first agreed on. Clyde and Bonnie had changed the date.[8]

Floyd and Mullins met Clyde and Bonnie at Lancaster, Texas. Clyde and Bonnie were traveling in a 1934 V-8 Ford Coupe, and Floyd was in a Model-A Ford Coupe. The group went to Corsicana, Texas, and left Floyd's car in a garage. Everyone then went to the Eastham Farm in Clyde's V-8 Coupe, arriving around one or two o'clock Sunday morning. When they got there they drove about two miles from the farm, and Clyde and Bonnie waited while Floyd and Mullins hid the guns. After they hid the guns they returned to Corsicana, leaving Floyd there. Mullins, Clyde, and Bonnie went back to the Eastham Farm and drove around on the roads. Floyd was to visit Raymond Hamilton that Sunday afternoon.

The Sunday before the Tuesday morning break, Prison Manager B. B. Monzingo saw Floyd Hamilton in the office of the Eastham Farm. Floyd came there and registered to see his brother, Raymond.[9]

The trio saw Floyd later on Sunday afternoon. Floyd had told Raymond where the guns were, and he told Floyd that the squads were working at the same place.[10] On Sunday and Monday, Mullins, Clyde, and Bonnie came back down in the river bottoms near Eastham and drove around on the back roads.

Ninety-six-year-old Mrs. Monzingo has lived in Lovelady, Texas almost all her life. She worked in the town bank before it collapsed financially, like so many others in the 1930s. Later she taught school in the little town near Eastham prison. Many people in town relied on the prison for work. One story she recalls was the local rumor of where Bonnie and Clyde were the night before the Eastham Raid.

> They didn't know who they were at the time. They found out later, the Bum Strange family, that is. I guess they must have been waiting or something. A long time getting out 'cause they were pooped out, and they slept awhile at this negro man's house. They are all dead. All of the ones that would know are all dead. They just rested there or ate there or something, and when they left they gave one of the children a dollar and they said they thought they were one of the nicest people they ever saw.

Mullins said it differently. He said the group slept in the car, but not at the same time.[11] On Monday they again drove around, and then on Tuesday morning they went to Calhoun's Ferry Road near the Trinity River. They stopped the car at the edge of the woods. The line was going to work in those woods, and Joe Palmer and Raymond Hamilton were going to be in the *line.* The group stopped the car at about six-thirty or seven o'clock in the morning. The rescue squad had four automatic pistols, four sawed-off shot guns and two Browning high-powered rifles (BARs). The BARs would shoot twenty shots, and they had plenty of ammunition for them.[12]

Some other guards in the area that day were J. B. McCafferty, Britt Matthews, Ed Frizzell, and Bobby Bullard. On January 16, the morning of the break, Raymond Hamilton was supposed to be in Number Two Squad, but instead was in Number One. Guard Olin Bozeman had Number One Squad, and Mr. Bishop had Number Two Squad. Raymond Hamilton was supposed to be in Bishop's squad.[13]

In the meantime, other activities were going on in Old Eastham. Plow Squad One was starting to line up in the main hall for work detail. Hugh Kennedy was in the first slot, and the bosses were outside getting ready for a head count. Plow Squad Two started to line up, the squad Ray Hamilton was assigned to be in, but he wasn't with them. Kennedy had felt strange all morning. The routine wasn't the same.

"I've got a bad count!" someone yelled outside the door. "Plow One has one too many!" Kennedy was hit in the back, the result of a scuffle right behind him. He turned to see what the problem was, and as he did, Hamilton shoved a homemade knife through the back of a convict who was in Plow One. Hamilton then pulled the knife out and buried it in the man's back again, throwing him to the ground. As Plow Squad One started to march forward, two steps apart, the count was correct as Hamilton slipped behind Kennedy with a cap with side flaps partially covering his face.[14]

No one in the line looked like the people they were when they first came to Eastham. Their skin was dark from chopping cotton, or miscellaneous tasks. They were skinny from working dawn to dusk outside. On the inside, convicts became cannibalistic piranha, abusing, raping, and terrorizing each other, as though the guards' abuses were not enough.

The line pushed forward toward the woodpiles on that foggy morning. It was time to gather the wood that had been cut until near dark the day before. Again things were strange. Major Crowson, the highrider, was with the squads. *Crowson always rode far away from the line, never with them going out,* Kennedy thought. He remembered the beatings Crowson was so eager to give the prisoners. The guards carried a rubber tube with a broomstick inside of it to hit the convicts when they didn't like something that was going on in the field or the dormitory. Joe Palmer definitely got his share of licks, because he lagged behind the rest of the squad due to illness. If that stick hit a man in the head the right way, it would knock him unconscious. That was the whole point of it.

Normally, Crowson would ride far to the right or the left of the line until he got to the edge of the woods. Then he would do something strange. The highrider, called that because his job as an expert shot was to hide somewhere in the woods so he could pick off an escape attempt, would put one hand on the saddle horn and the other in a spread web across his face so nobody knew who he was looking at in any given time. Others called him "Long arm" because of the .30-30 rifle he had on his saddle. The squads had their own nickname for him.

They gotta' know Ray is right behind me in the wrong squad, Kennedy thought. Two steps behind, to be exact. The line had walked over a mile, and despite the fog, Kennedy knew it wouldn't be long before they reached the woodpiles they had stacked last evening. Eight-foot-high, tepee-style stacks had been made all across the front of the woods. They got closer to the woods. The stacks became visible. A sweat started from the march, even though it was mid-January. No one was allowed to take care of restroom duties inside of Eastham itself in the morning, so those who needed to relieve themselves did so in the woods before work started. Kennedy didn't care, because he had secretly been going to the bathroom inside for quite a while. It made him feel less powerless to do something that the guards didn't know about.

Kennedy had been having a problem with a particular guard, and the last thing he wanted was to catch a ride on the barrel. That was a punishment his already swollen feet could do without. The woodpile got closer. He thought back to when Bud Russell brought him to Eastham with a shackle around his ankles and waist, cuffs on his wrist, metal loop around his neck, and a ride to the Burning 'Ham. It especially hurt because he had partially grown up at Russell's house, not far from his home in Whitney, Texas. He even owned one of "Uncle Bud's" rings.[15]

Some men had axes, some didn't, as they approached the woodpiles. That is when something else strange happened. Someone gave a command for all but Plow One to veer toward the right, heading for an empty field. Guard Bozeman called Major Crowson to help him. It was finally acknowledged that Ray Hamilton had jumped squad. No one was allowed to go past Kennedy in the cadence of the squad, but as they approached the woodpile Hamilton sprung·forward past the lead man. There was a red handkerchief on top of a woodpile next to Squad One, and Hamilton rapidly walked toward it. Bozeman and Crowson were nearby.[16]

Bozeman had Squad One the morning of the break. The guard had seen Hamilton jump squad as soon as he came out the door, but it was customary to take them on out to the field and change after they got out there. Working around two miles from the building wasn't the easiest thing to do. The squads were cutting wood, in *throughs* about twenty-five steps wide. There were several squads of men out there. Each squad would take a through of about twenty-five steps. When Bozeman got out there to where the squad was set to work, Crowson started to ride off. Bozeman called to him, and he came to where Bozeman was at.

"Tell the captain to come and get Raymond Hamilton and put him back in the squad he belongs in," Bozeman told the highrider.

"All right, you better watch him," was the reply. "Yes sir, boy, you had better look out, that means something." Bozeman and Crowson's horses were sitting side by side. They could have reached out and touched each other.[17] Both men were facing west, Crowson being on Bozeman's lefthand side.[18]

Joe Palmer started to walk toward Bozeman, turned suddenly at Crowson and said, "All right." Then he gut-shot the highrider with a .45 caliber pistol at point-blank range.[19] Bozeman dropped over his horse, and Palmer shot at the guard's gun. Three or four bullets hit his gun. Hamilton went to the base of the woodpile, pulled a .45 pistol from the middle of the stack, and ran toward guard Bozeman. He then grabbed the neck of Bozeman's horse, swung around to the other side, and fired at the guard.[20] The horse wheeled and a bullet hit Bozeman's hand, and then a shot went through the back of his saddle, the bullet hitting Bozeman in the hip. Mullins later swore in court Hamilton's gun had been fired.[21]

Bozeman could see a car off in the distance, and he could make out one person inside the vehicle when a horn started to blast. When the horn blew, Bozeman fired his shotgun one time. He tried to fire at Joe Palmer.

Crowson yelled, "My God!" after he was shot. Joe Palmer continued to shoot at Bozeman, finally shooting the gun out of his hands. Crowson's horse wheeled and Bozeman's also wheeled. Bozeman then went toward Eastham. Major Crowson began going on down through the woods in the opposite direction from the camp. Bozeman didn't know how many shots had been fired when his horse wheeled and ran off.[22]

Guard Bullard was not far off with Squad Six when the gunfire started. Actually, he was pretty close to Olin Bozeman, about twenty-five yards from where the shooting was going on.[23] Kennedy reflected decades later that Bullard was much farther away, but Bullard remembered differently.

When he saw Joe Palmer shooting at Bozeman and Crowson, he leveled his shotgun and tried to kill Palmer. His horse also wheeled after he shot, and he jumped off the horse and got behind a woodpile, holding his men from running away.[24]

"Follow me!" Hamilton yelled to Kennedy. "I'm not following you anywhere," was Kennedy's reply. Hamilton headed for the woods. Almost simultaneously, Hilton Bybee and Henry Methvin ran for the woods. Methvin was serving a ten-year sentence for a September 20, 1930, attempted murder and car theft of a Refugio County man, Charles Hughes.[25]

Joe Palmer was dressed in stripes, the sign of an escapee, troublemaker, or parole violator. He took off into the woods. Hamilton yelled to Clyde and Mullins, "Give us something else!"[26] There was a little opening just before they got to the fence, and Mullins could see the men running toward the ditch. Palmer and Hamilton both had .45 army pistols, the pistols Mullins and Floyd helped hide on the farm. Mullins knew one of those pistols well, because Clyde had possessed it ever since he had gotten away in Missouri.[27]

French ran into the woods, but in a different direction. All hell broke loose when Clyde and Mullins then opened up with BAR machine guns in the distance over Kennedy's head. Small branches and leaves started to fall around him as bullets cut through the surroundings. He stood there watching what was going on around him.[28] Crowson started to ride toward the woods in apparent bewilderment, then turned toward Eastham. Bozeman bolted his horse toward Eastham, but in a different path.[29] There were bullets ricocheting, and some prisoners dropped to the ground while others ran away.[30] When the convicts came to the car, four of the escapees got in the rear end of the car, and they started for Dallas. There is argument as to who said who could go and who must stay behind when the men got to the get-away car. What is known is who did climb into the car that morning. Clyde Barrow, Bonnie Parker, Raymond Hamilton, Joe Palmer, Hilton Bybee, James Mullins, and Henry Methvin.

Brew Hubbard was moving a cow that morning on the Calhoun road when he heard three or four pistol shots and then a shotgun blast. Immediately afterward there was a rain of shots. The last shots were too fast for either a pistol or a shotgun. He looked around and saw four or five men come to a car at the bridge on the road, one man wearing striped prison clothes.[31] When Joe Palmer got to the gate, he pulled off his shirt and left it and his hat there. The car started off and went about twenty or thirty feet, and someone in the car told Hubbard to move on. The convicts thought at first that he was a prison guard.[32]

"He is all right. He is a negro; he hasn't got anything," someone else said, and then the car continued down the road, passing the man within ten feet. Palmer cursed the man for being in the way as the getaway car passed, sitting in the turtle back and still holding a .45 pistol. The car continued in the direction of Weldon.[33] The car took off at a high rate of speed, Palmer still wearing striped pants.[34]

The rest of the convicts back at the woodpiles just looked at each other and then started to walk unguarded back toward the prison.[35] First, they sat around and smoked cigarettes for about an hour, deciding what to do. *Murder house, just plain murder house.* Before the night was over, several members of the squad were beaten just for being there, and in the middle of the night an unaccounted-for convict was brought in by guards; he was shot to death.[36] Captain Monzingo was furious, and no dinner was given that night.

From there the car full of escaped convicts traveled toward Weldon as planned. After they traveled about a mile past Weldon, they stopped. Joe Palmer had been knocked out from the gasoline exhaust of the car, so they put him in the front of the car riding in Mullins' lap. Soon after that Joe Palmer woke and started to talk about the break, stating that he had shot two guards (Bozeman was also shot in the hand). He said they were Olin Bozeman and Major Crowson.[37]

Prison Manager Monzingo was at his Eastham office when

Crowson rode up on his horse. "I've been shot," Crowson told
him. The Steward, Mr. Cline, walked up to the two men. "Go get
your car and take him to the hospital," the manager told Cline.[38]
He left to go get a car, and at some time near that period
Bozeman arrived because they were taken to the hospital in the
same car.[39] Gordon Burns was the Notary Public for Walker
County in Huntsville. He went to see Crowson in Huntsville's
Memorial Hospital on the night of January 23, 1934. That was
seven days after his gunshot wound at Eastham, and the highrider was not faring well. In the presence of Lee Simmons and
doctor W. B. Veazey, Burns took a dying statement from
Crowson.[40] The statement read:

> The State of Texas, County of Walker. I, Major J. Crowson,
> being of sound mind and memory do hereby make this my
> dying declaration, to Gordon M. Burns, Notary Public in and
> for Walker County, Texas, and at the time of making this
> dying declaration I am conscious of approaching death and I
> believe there is no hope of me recovering, and I am making
> this statement voluntarily and not through the persuasion of
> any person and that this declaration is not made in answer to
> interrogatories to lead me and I am telling the truth, the
> whole truth and nothing but the truth, so HELP ME GOD:
>
> My name is Major J. Crowson. I am called at the Eastham
> State Prison Farm "Long Arm Man" or "Backfield Man," and
> on the morning of January 16, 1934, Olin Bozeman was carry-
> ing No. 1 squad. I was riding a horse and I was in front of
> Bozeman's squad. It was about 7:15 A.M. when Bozeman called
> me and said, "Raymond Hamilton has jumped in my squad,"
> and I said, "Boy, that is for something," and Bozeman said,
> "Yes it is." Joe Palmer was in Boss Bozeman's squad, and he
> pulled an automatic pistol. It was a .44 or .45, and Joe Palmer
> shot me in the stomach. After Joe Palmer shot me in the stom-
> ach he shot at me once while I was riding away. When Joe
> Palmer pulled his gun on me, Joe Palmer said, "Don't you boys
> try to do anything." I never did get my hand on my gun, and I
> never did shoot at Joe Palmer who shot me.
>
> Witness my hand at Huntsville, Texas, this the 23rd
> January, 1934.
>
> (Signed) M. J. Crowson
> Witnesses:
> Lee Simmons
> W. B. Veazey, M.D.[41]

The nurse propped the mortally wounded man up in bed. After the Notary recorded the declaration and Crowson signed it, he began talking to the three men in the room.

"Colonel Simmons, Joe Palmer shot me in cold blood. He didn't give me a dog's chance. Colonel Simmons, I hope you catch him and put him in the electric chair."[42] Major Crowson died on January 27, 1934, and was taken home.[43]

Doctor Veazey treated Major Crowson from January 16 until the morning of January 27 for his gunshot wound. The doctor noticed that the wound on his body was about the size of a .45 bullet. The exit wound was about two inches higher than the entrance. In sworn testimony, Veazey described Crowson's condition and his death from complications from pneumonia:

> He had a complication of the lower lobe of the right lung, near the abdomen, called pneumonia. For the pneumonia, I administered electrical heat and gave him a blood transfusion, and I did use some oxygen, but it didn't seem to help him any. That was the day he was taken sick, I believe. He had been in the hospital six days before he developed pneumonia. His temperature was not normal. It rose steadily on Monday night, the 22nd. His temperature had been running around 102 and 103, and it rose to 105 that night. I had to give him ether in the operation. The pneumonia contributed to bring about his death, but the gunshot wound was the communicating cause of the pneumonia. That limited his breathing on that side. He didn't get as much air in there as he should have had around his abdomen.[44]
>
> As to the nature of the operation that we performed that morning, we opened his abdomen. I opened his abdomen because I wasn't sure that his intestines were punctured by the bullet. The intestines were punctured. They were badly shot up. It was necessary to remove a portion of his intestines. As well as I remember, one place in the intestines had four holes in it and it couldn't be sutured and still kept there, and it had to be removed, it was so badly torn. Ordinarily a man shot through the intestines is a mortally wounded man, and the chances are strongly against his getting well.[45]

However, another doctor, Doctor Anderson, had also seen Crowson's condition. In his sworn testimony, he stated:

As to whether or not Major Crowson died of gunshot wounds
or of pneumonia, in my opinion if it had not been for the
pneumonia he would have gotten well, and therefore I would
say that the final cause of his death was pneumonia.[46] The
pneumonia was the primary cause of his death, and the gunshot wound was the primary cause of the pneumonia, the
cause that brought it about.[47]

Mrs. Monzingo looked at the clock on the wall again in her
Lovelady home. A friend was ill, and she was waiting for a phone
call. She then changed her glance to look out the window, recall-
ing events from sixty-four years ago. She said:

> I remember sitting at the window when he was being
> buried. Major Crowson was a barber here in town before he
> went to work for the prison. I remember standing at the win-
> dow watching the funeral procession go. It was a large proces-
> sion because it was quite an unusual thing for that to happen
> like that. The people in town were opposed to Bonnie and
> Clyde. That was a horrible thing, they thought. My Uncle
> Craig gave the blood for the Major's transfusion.
> I knew it was bad for us after the escape because we
> couldn't cut our hair, and we were seven girls. We couldn't cut
> our hair because Bonnie Parker bobbed her hair. Ben
> Monzingo was related to my husband. He ran the prison there
> for a few years. Everyone hated Ben Monzingo that had ever
> been around a penitentiary, you know. That was when they
> whipped them and so forth.

It was arranged for Hugh Kennedy to be transferred to the
Walls Unit in Huntsville for safekeeping after he was interviewed by prison authorities and the Walker County District
Attorney, Max Rogers. It wouldn't be any good for the state in
court if someone murdered the eyewitness before he could testify against Ray Hamilton. For some reason, Kennedy was never
called as a witness and finished his sentence at the Walls.[48]
Lee Simmons had promised Major Crowson in the hospital
that he would not let them get away with what they had done,
and Crowson's father reminded him of that promise at his son's
funeral. Crowson had felt that he disobeyed orders by not staying out of range.[49] Simmons fired and blacklisted two of the
Eastham guards who ran away instead of staying to fight. The

prison superintendent thought the men had violated their oaths, and despite the intervention of State Senator Patton and Representative Daniel on the men's behalf, he would not budge on the issue.[50]

The players of the Eastham Raid were desperate men capable of anything, as they had already proved. With nothing to lose at this point, Texas braced for the Pandora's box that had been opened that winter morning. However, these men had earned a powerful enemy in Lee Simmons, and they would learn that he had powerful allies, including an ex–Texas Ranger named Frank Hamer. It became personal for both sides on January 16, 1934, and no quarter had been called.

CHAPTER 11

The Getaway

I was supposed to get $2,000 for putting those guns there on the farm, and I got about $685. Raymond Hamilton paid me that. Joe Palmer was present in the crowd when I got $500 of it.[1] That was on the January 26 after the break had happened on the January 16. That was between Boyd and Rhome, out close to Denton. There was in the bunch at that time, myself, Floyd Hamilton, Raymond Hamilton, Clyde Barrow, Bonnie Parker, and Henry Methvin. Floyd and I were in one car and we stopped. One car was in bad circumstances. We had three cars.[2]

— James Mullins' testimony for the State at Joe Palmer's murder trial in Anderson, Texas

Roadblocks sprang up in towns between Crockett and Dallas, but Clyde Barrow left the main road after Eastham and drove through farm fields to escape detection. Reaching Hillsboro, he stopped for gas. The attendant at the station was very excited about something as he approached the getaway car.

"Did you hear about Raymond Hamilton escaping from prison?" he asked.

"No," replied Barrow, "really?"

"Clyde and Bonnie just walked right into the dining room this morning and took Ray out while everybody was eating!"[3] Another version of the story is that the station attendant, not realizing his customers' identities, told Barrow that Bonnie and Clyde shot their way right in to the Eastham cell house and freed Raymond Hamilton. Barrow acted amazed at the story as he paid the attendant.[4] That's how fast these fabrications got started.

The entire Southwest was on alert for this carload of escaped convicts, but Clyde drove the back roads toward Rhome, Texas. The plan was to meet with Floyd Hamilton and L. C. Barrow, one of Clyde's brothers. By the time the carload reached Joplin, Missouri, plans had been made. They continued on to Rembrandt, Iowa, in the far northwest corner of the state. Palmer, Methvin, and Bybee had previously agreed to help Raymond raise the one thousand dollars owed to James Mullins by robbing a bank as soon after the break as possible.[5]

Joe Palmer was having one of his very bad sick spells by the time the group drove into town. Palmer was too sick to walk, much less be any good in a bank robbery, so he slept on the floorboard in the back seat of the car. In the meantime, Hamilton, Methvin, and Bybee went inside the bank and robbed it. Even though Joe didn't participate in the robbery, Barrow, Bybee, and Methvin agreed that Joe should be given an equal share of the $3,800 loot. Raymond Hamilton objected, which was exactly his nature in most instances that involved money. Clyde stood his ground on the subject, and Hamilton gave up and agreed to the split.[6]

Shortly after the Rembrandt heist, Hilton Bybee struck out on his own. On Tuesday, January 30, Bybee was arrested in Amarillo. Bybee had spent his brief freedom in Oklahoma and the Texas Panhandle.[7] It was back to Eastham for the man who shot Ernest Slape in the back for grins.

The remaining members of the newly recruited Barrow Gang drove to Houston. Joe Palmer had a good memory when it came to paying back injustices done to him. Just as he went out of his way to gut-shoot Major Crowson for the beatings he [had] received from the highrider, Joe had business to settle with an Eastham building tender named Wade. It was Wade who was directly responsible for many severe whippings of Joe. This building tender enjoyed the torture and pain he could inflict or have inflicted on other convicts in Eastham. In Houston, Palmer found an attorney and gave him a large sum of money to ensure Wade's release from prison. Within days of his release, Wade was abducted and driven to East Texas. Wade was shot to death and left in the woods thirty miles north of Marshall. Joe drew a map and mailed it to the famous prison reform newspaperman, Harry McCormick. The attached note read, "Here's where you'll find a rat."[8]

After the Wade incident, the Barrow Gang drove to Missouri. Hamilton decided to test the waters of command by complaining that things would be much better if he was in charge. Joe Palmer was in the middle of one of his illness spells and had grown to detest everything about Hamilton, not the least being Ray's role as an informant at Eastham. The last thing he wanted to listen to was Ray's whining. "Punk blabber-mouth braggart," Palmer suddenly hissed at Ray as he stared at him. Ray turned red but did not respond. Palmer pulled the covers over his head and tried to sleep. Minutes later Hamilton drew a pistol, as if to shoot Palmer while he was sleeping. Clyde saw what was about to happen and he reached into the back seat and slapped Ray across the face. The result was Clyde losing control of the car, missing a curve and driving into a ditch. One of the wheels was broken and they had to steal another car to continue on to Joplin. When the gang got to Joplin, Clyde went to the front of the Conner Hotel. Palmer got out of the car. He was starting to feel worse than he had before the wreck, and there was no way he could be near Hamilton anymore. Clyde told Joe he would come back for him in four to six weeks, and the Barrow Gang left.[9]

On Monday, February 19, Clyde and Raymond burglarized the National Guard Armory at Ranger, Texas. The total haul included several Browning automatic rifles (BARs), Colt .45 automatic pistols, and ammunition into the rear of their stolen V-8.[10] By mid-February the gang's resources were depleted and they had time to visit relatives and friends in North Texas. Hamilton had been in hiding in Wichita Falls, where he had attached to his ex-crime partner's wife, Mary O'Dare. Gene had been sent to prison and Mary had always liked Ray. Mary was despised by everyone but Raymond in the Barrow Gang, but he was determined to have her by his side.

Hamilton and Mary met with members of the gang near Vernon, Texas. Hamilton and Barrow made battle plans, and on February 19 Henry Methvin, Joe Palmer, Raymond Hamilton, Clyde Barrow, Bonnie Parker, and Mary O'Dare left Vernon to meet near Greenville with members of the Barrow and Parker families. After that the gang loaded up and headed for Ranger, where they burglarized yet another National Guard armory and got the usual cache of weapons and ammunition. The next day the gang met Raymond's brother Floyd on the Lancaster Highway, and during the family meeting earlier there was a secret agenda by the gang; a casing of the Lancaster Bank.

The following day, Raymond, Clyde, and Joe Palmer drove into Lancaster and parked on a side street near the R. P. Henry Bank. Palmer stayed in the car while Hamilton and Barrow got out and walked into the building, surprising the cashier and the lone customer in the bank. Barrow showed a sawed-off shotgun, while Ray had a tow sack tied to his belt to gather the money. Hamilton pushed the customer aside as Barrow hurried to the back of the bank. There was another customer, Bud Brooks, in the bank when the bandit burst through the door. He didn't notice them because he was reading a newspaper. The customers were forced to sit on the floor as the cashier opened the safe drawer. While Clyde kept everyone at bay with the shotgun, Raymond collected $4,138.50 in the sack. The victims were then forced out the back door, and the robbers ran for the getaway car. Joe Palmer had the role of getaway driver, and before anyone could do anything he sped away, all bandits safe with a tow sack full of cash.

After leaving the Lancaster robbery, they headed to the Bluebird Farm, where Bonnie, Methvin, and Mary were waiting on the Wilmer Road. The holdup car had been stolen from G. Jeff Waggoner of Wichita Falls, and it was abandoned for a car stolen from the Earle Johnson Motor Company of Temple. After making the switch to the Ford sedan, the outlaws drove to the Oklahoma line. Raymond, seated in the back with Mary and the guns, wanted to start dividing the loot. Barrow agreed. Hamilton went to work, splitting the money into three equal parts.

"What about me?" asked Mary.

"You get nothing," snapped Barrow. While the group mo-

tored toward one of their old hideaways in southeastern Okla-
homa, Clyde, who was driving, noticed in the rearview mirror that
Raymond, in the back seat, was cutting Mary in on a share of the
Lancaster money. Hamilton was up to his old tricks, and as usual
Clyde had to intervene. The theft had netted Barrow and
Hamilton $4,176.

"Ray, she don't get none of that," Barrow complained. "It's
split between Bonnie and me and you. She didn't do a damned
thing."

"Hell, neither did Bonnie," Raymond challenged. "She's my
girl—she gets a cut." Mary ended up getting part of the money,
but it was less than a fourth.[11]

Raymond slid a handful of cash onto Mary's lap. Clyde, who
had been watching everything carefully in the rearview mirror, was
enraged. He pulled over and searched Hamilton, finding an extra
six hundred dollars on him. "Ditch Mary right now, or get out,"
Barrow snapped.

That was enough for Raymond Hamilton. On March 6, 1934,
he stole a car and told Mary to get in and wait for him. Hamilton
said his goodbyes to Clyde and Bonnie and left.[12] Barrow said
nothing. He could not have been more pleased. He was finally rid
of the "washerwoman," Mary O'Dare.[13] The Barrow Gang worked
their way back to Dallas.

Several days later, Raymond Hamilton also returned to
Texas. On March 19 he and Floyd robbed the Grand Prairie State
Bank of $1,543.74. On March 31 Raymond and Mary O'Dare got
$1,867.74 from the State National Bank of West, Texas.[14]

On Friday, March 23, Hilton Bybee's name showed up again
after he escaped from the Houston County jail in Crockett. After
his arrest in Amarillo, he was accused of being one of the gunmen
that murdered Major Crowson during the Eastham Raid, and he
was set to stand trial for the charge. Fortunately for Bybee, two
days before his escape Crowson had given his dying statement and
the charge had been dismissed. Hilton Bybee was captured by officers near Woodson in West Texas and jailed in Breckenridge.
Hilton Bybee was sentenced to twenty-five years' imprisonment on
Sunday, April 8, 1934, by a district court jury. He was convicted of
robbery with firearms and kidnapping in connection with the
filling station holdup in March.

In the meantime, Joe Palmer had gotten back together with the group after Hamilton left and had thumbed a ride to Dallas so the Barrow and Parker families would know the location of an Easter meeting Bonnie and Clyde wanted to have with their kin. Joe went to Emma Parker's house but he found no one home. He then went to the Star Service Station but only found Clyde's dad, Henry. Palmer decided to wait around for awhile as Henry attended to waiting customers.[15]

North of Grapevine, Bonnie, Clyde, and Henry also waited.[16] A rabbit hopped leisurely beside the road, munching blades of grass and playing quietly. This rabbit was a surprise Bonnie wanted to give her mother. Clyde was glad to get rid of it. As the gang was dodging the law, Bonnie insisted they pull over and bathe the rabbit in a roadside creek, half freezing the animal. Methvin sat alone. Barrow was stretched out on the back seat trying to get some much-needed sleep. While waiting for family members, Bonnie and Henry drank whiskey. Clyde was not drinking. He had heard Hamilton had robbed the West bank and knew the lawmen might be in the area searching for him.

Around three-thirty in the afternoon, Bonnie looked toward the highway. Three highway patrolmen were driving slowly past the entrance to the dirt road. They took a long look at the black V-8 with canary yellow wheels and then split up. Two of the officers, E. B. Wheeler and H. D. Murphy, made a wide circle on their motorcycles, as if to turn around. The third patrolman, Polk Ivy, continued on toward Roanoke.[17] Bonnie grabbed the rabbit and walked back to the car to wake Clyde. Barrow rubbed his eyes and saw the two motorcycles. With a sawed-off shotgun hidden behind him, he moved from the back seat and to the open car door. Henry Methvin, not used to Clyde's way of doing things, was already aware of the officers and gripping a Browning automatic rifle. "Let's take them," said Clyde as the motorcycles got close to the group.[18] What Barrow meant was to kidnap them and joy ride with them. That's not the way Methvin understood it, and in all fairness to Methvin, it seems that when Clyde Barrow said to "take them," it would mean to kill someone.

E. B. Wheeler, twenty-six, was in front of his twenty-two-year-old partner, H. D. Murphy. It was obvious to Clyde that

neither lawman sensed any danger—their side arms were plainly holstered. When Wheeler drew within ten feet of the car,
Barrow started to leap into view and get the drop on both officers. To his surprise, however, Methvin opened fire, striking
Wheeler in the chest with a line of steel-jacketed slugs. Murphy
was on his first day of service when he saw the four-year veteran
shot off his motorcycle. Murphy got off his bike and fished two
shotgun shells from his pocket. The patrolman started to reach
for the sawed-off shotgun strapped to the rear fender of his
machine. One can almost see Barrow shake his head at knowing
he had to kill this man. He hesitated but then saw that the patrolman intended to fight, so he raised his weapon and fired
three rounds. When the smoke cleared, both lawmen were dead
and lying in the dirt.[19] Clyde was mad enough at Henry to kill
him for his reckless action, and he had a few words with Henry
as he swore at him for his folly. Before Ivy knew what had befall-
en his fellow officers, Barrow was speeding toward Oklahoma.[20]

Raymond Hamilton's new car didn't have a radio, so he
didn't know about the situation at Grapevine. As he drove into
West Dallas that Sunday afternoon, he let Mary out near Floyd
Hamilton's house, and she told Floyd to meet Raymond near
Grapevine. (Some sources say Barrow was waiting for Raymond
to kill him because of letters written to newspapers after the split
that said he was a bank robber while Clyde was a nickel and
dime thief.) When Mary told Floyd where Raymond planned to
meet him she talked about the yellow wheels on the car, and the
elder brother nearly fainted. The meeting place was only about
a mile from where the shootings occurred, and Barrow's car also
had yellow tires. Floyd managed to get to his brother before the
law did, and Floyd told Raymond about the murders. The
brothers changed the wheels on their cars so Raymond would
not be driving with the yellow ones that officers were looking for
in the area.

Raymond Hamilton drove to New Orleans and stole another car immediately. He then registered at the Lafayette Hotel
and lived the good life with Mary, buying her jewelry and
clothes.[21] Following the Easter killings, Bonnie and Clyde and
Henry Methvin went to eastern Oklahoma, East Texas, and
Louisiana. The Louisiana trip would be the end of Bonnie and

Clyde, and Joe Palmer knew early on that he didn't want to go there. It would prove to be an ugly treachery, and Clyde had several times told people that one of his own would eventually cost him his life.[22]

Hamilton had decided at this point to hit the railroads again, and somehow being broke, ragged, and sunburned, he rode the suspension cables of a boxcar for nearly two weeks. He had parted company with Mary O'Dare, the washerwoman, in New Orleans. Along the way he became friends with a hobo named Teddy. Hamilton couldn't let his lifestyle go, and he convinced Teddy to help him rob the First National Bank in Lewisville, thirty miles north of Dallas. At 2:45 P.M. on April 25, Hamilton and Teddy drove to the bank. It's funny how bank robbers decide what to wear when they rob a place. When the Whitey Walker Gang robbed banks in the oil-rich Texas Panhandle, they wore suits. When they robbed Central and East Texas banks they wore overalls with four-day-growth beards on their face. In pictures the Barrow Gang are dressed superbly, despite the country dirt roads and gunfights. Raymond Hamilton knew what he was doing as well, and when he hit the Lewisville Bank he was dressed in a dirty, wrinkled shirt. He quickly went inside the bank while Teddy waited as a getaway driver in the car.[23]

Hamilton got the money available behind the teller's cages, but then he found out that the vault had a time lock. "Ain't that a mess?" scoffed Raymond. "That's the trouble with Texas, all the banks are on time locks!" He then ran out of the building.

Going north on Highway 75 near McKinney, the robbers made good time in their getaway. It's too bad phone calls traveled faster; that is another reason many bank robbers either took hostages or locked witnesses in the vault. After a few phone calls, there was a massive roadblock near Howe. Still traveling north, Hamilton spotted Gray County Deputy McDaniel coming toward him in the southbound lane. Before the deputy knew it, Ray's car had flown past him. The deputy whirled his car around and topped eighty miles per hour as he raced through the little town of Howe after Hamilton. Ray saw the roadblock almost too late north of town. He slammed on the brakes and made a 180-degree turn in the middle of the road, but Deputy McDaniel swerved in front of the outlaw's car and forced Ray to the side of the road. A member of the posse jumped from the car and pointed a Thompson submachine gun on the two bandits. The two emerged from the Chevy with their hands held high. "I suppose you know who you've got," said Ray.

"Raymond . . . ?" the man asked.

"You damned right!" the fugitive said. "Raymond Hamilton!"[24]

The following afternoon, Ray was reunited with his brother, Floyd, who had been picked up two weeks earlier as an accomplice in the raid on Eastham.

Just before Ray Hamilton's arrest, the rest of the gang had located Joe Palmer in Joplin. Palmer had gone to Missouri from Dallas as soon as he heard about the mess in Grapevine. The gang of Methvin, Barrow, Parker, and Palmer went to a farm in Louisiana. Bonnie and Clyde had been using an abandoned farmhouse ten miles south of Gibsland, Louisiana, as a hideout. At the hideout Clyde gave Joe two pistols.[25]

Once again crisscrossing the Midwest, Clyde, Joe, and Henry robbed a Sac City, Iowa, bank. The total haul of the bank heist was $2,800. Bonnie waited outside of town with a backup car.[26] After the Iowa bank robbery, Barrow wanted to settle down in Louisiana. Joe wanted nothing to do with the idea, preferring to take his cut of the loot and return to the Conner Hotel in Joplin.[27] Palmer wanted to go to the World's Fair, and Clyde was ready to get back home and hide out for awhile.[28] The group separated, and the next time Palmer would be near Clyde Barrow was when he went to his funeral, still on the run from the law, probably wearing the suit Bonnie had bought him as a present in Memphis, Tennessee.[29]

What exactly did or did not happen in Louisiana those last few days will probably never be known. What is known is that Henry Methvin, Clyde Barrow, and Bonnie Parker stopped in front of the Majestic Café in Shreveport and sent Methvin in for a few sandwiches. While they waited, a police car cruised past Bonnie and Clyde. Methvin was seated at the inside counter and didn't notice, intentionally or otherwise.

Clyde drove away, fearful of being spotted by the policeman in the patrol car. Oddly, just as soon as the outlaw's car was gone, Methvin calmly rose from his stool and stepped to the door. Moving out to the sidewalk, he glanced both ways, then strolled off down the street, leaving the sandwiches and drinks on the counter. Clyde had an understanding with Henry that in the event of a situation like this they were to meet again at the Cole place, the hideout they had been using in the woods near Gibsland. Clyde took his time getting back to the hideout. Maybe it was his reported sixth sense of traps, or maybe he wanted to go somewhere else first, but he didn't head toward the hideout until a day after they had separated from Henry. Strangely, that was about the same amount of time a group of men with machine guns lay in a mosquito-infested roadside in the wait of an ambush.

At 8:00 A.M. on May 23, 1934, a stolen tan V-8 pulled up in front of Canfield's Café in the hamlet of Gibsland, ten miles northeast of the hideout. Bonnie was wearing a bright red dress with matching shoes and hat. Clyde wore a silk suit, a blue western-style shirt, and a tie. After donuts and coffee, the couple ordered two sandwiches to go and returned to the car. Clyde took off his shoes like he usually did when he was driving. He slid the barrel of a 16-gauge sawed-off shotgun between his left leg and the car door, and a 20-gauge shotgun rested against his right leg.[30]

It would be the last time the Southwest's number-one-wanted outlaws would have to worry about the necessary positioning of their weapons. Death was waiting nearby. A group of lawmen that were ragged, fatigued, mosquito bitten, and perhaps a bit edgy that their targets may actually show up for the finish of a long and deadly game were deciding whether to stay or call it a day. As Clyde drove at top speed down the country road, he saw Iverson Methvin's truck in the distance. Iverson was Henry's father.

Clyde let his car coast about five hundred yards toward a shallow valley at the base of two small hills. The truck was on top of the first hill, and was strangely facing north in the southbound lane. The truck had been jacked up, and the left front wheel had been removed and was laying in the middle of the gravel road. Looking at Bonnie and Clyde's Ford coming toward him near the truck was Iverson Methvin. Barrow drew alongside the stricken truck and applied the brakes, shotguns still in place on either side of his legs. Bonnie took one last bite of her sandwich and placed it on a nickel-plated Colt .45 automatic that lay beneath a magazine she had on her lap. The pistol was cocked and ready to hand to Clyde if he needed it. Suddenly, the old man clutched his abdomen and ran to the edge of the woods as if he was going to get sick. Clyde straightened up and looked down the road; a northbound pulp wood truck was very slowly topping the second hill less than a quarter of a mile away. Clyde was blocking the road, so he depressed the clutch, shifted to first, and started to pull out of the workmen's way. Bonnie looked over to Clyde and spotted a man rising from behind a brush less than twenty feet from the car. She had to know what was about to happen next. A gun flashed, and five more men appeared from behind the pile . . .

Bonnie screamed and two shots tore out of a barrel in return. Over 120 steel-jacketed 30.06 slugs slammed into the driver's side of the V-8. The bullets ripped through both steel walls of the front door and the windshield with a tight grouping. The first two shots hit Barrow in the head.[31] More than twenty slugs hit Clyde's body as his foot slipped from the clutch pedal; eight bullets slammed through his spinal cord. The car began to wobble uncontrollably down the road as Bonnie's ninety-pound frame was ripped to pieces by at least twenty-eight shots, one blasting through the top of her head. Two more rounds crashed into the left side of her face, shattered her jaw, and crushed her teeth. Another tore several fingers from her right hand.[32]

As though the heavy fire power wasn't enough, two of the ambush men suddenly discarded their big weapons and drew .45 pistols as they leaped into the road chasing behind the car, firing several shots into its trunk. Alcorn called out for everyone to stop shooting, but no one heard him.[33]

One of the ambushers wanted to make sure everything was final, so he rushed down the hill and unloaded a machine gun into Bonnie's side of the car, riddling her body with shells. In all fairness, that is how scary the Barrow Gang was to the law enforcement community, to the public, to the whole damned world. It was like cutting a snake in half and not knowing if it could still strike back at you. The Barrow Gang would do what they needed to do at the drop of a hat. Many negative things have been said of Clyde Barrow. It has been said he was a Piggly Wiggly robber, and it is true that for the most part he did rob Ma and Pa establishments (although he never actually robbed a Piggly Wiggly). There is no doubt that Clyde Barrrow, who relied on his driving to get out of most problems, would rock and roll with the best of them. He hated police, and he was good with a BAR. It's that simple. People with a certain mindset do what they are going to do, and that's the end of it.

The stolen Warren car contained submachine guns, automatic shotguns, .45 automatic pistols (fourteen of them in all), and a thousand rounds of ammunition. When Clyde's body was removed from the car, the officers found $506.32 in his pockets, mostly in ten and twenty dollar bills.[34] In return for his father's betrayal of Bonnie and Clyde and helping in the ambush, Henry Methvin grabbed the coattails of Lee Simmons and secured a conditional pardon signed by governor Miriam "Ma" Ferguson.[35] That got rid of his ten-year sentence in Texas and gave him immunity from his other Texas crimes committed while on the run with Bonnie and Clyde. That didn't do him any good in Oklahoma, however. Lee Simmons wouldn't pull any strings for the outlaw in that state, and suddenly Methvin had to sweat a possible death sentence for the murder of Constable Cal Campbell at Commerce on April 6, 1934. Now that Clyde was dead, Henry was the only person associated with the crime. Oklahoma had no leniency for him, and he received a death sentence.[36]

In 1936 the Oklahoma Court of Appeals took Methvin's role in the ambush under consideration and commuted his sentence to life. Not everyone appreciated his role in betraying his friends, and Henry almost died after being stabbed in prison during the ten years he was behind bars.[37] After being released from the penitentiary he was pardoned by the governor. He probably should have stayed where he was, because on April 19, 1949, Henry's body was found near a railroad track, cut in half by a train.[38]

As for the rest of those involved in the raid, French was the first to be caught. He was in a different squad from the one in which the four men were working. When the disturbance started, he hid under a pile of brush and remained there while the chase was in progress. He tried to cross the Trinity River, but when he couldn't, he got lost in the woods. That's when the dogs came to help find him.[39]

French resigned himself to be a teacher of a music class and leader of the orchestra on the Retrieve State Farm. He was suspected of using narcotics and was transferred to the Walls Unit in Huntsville on February 12, 1938. French was returned to the Retrieve Farm on March 8, 1938, when he was suspected on having been involved in an escape attempt. He was involved in the digging of a trench for which an escape was supposed to be made from under the Walls. Although officials were unable to prove their case, French was returned to the Retrieve Farm.[40] He was discharged on September 29, 1940, from the Central State Farm. Oklahoma asked for him back, and that is all we know of French.

As for Hilton Bybee, he was charged with harboring a fugitive on February 15, 1935. Bybee wasn't the kind of man to sit back and watch the world go by, so he decided to escape. He made it, but not for long. On March, 28, 1934, Hilton Bybee and Cecil Lewis, alias Jimmy Welling, stole sixty-three army automatic pistols, .45 caliber, from the Texas National Guard armory at Jacksboro, Texas. The stickup man was shot and killed on July 2, 1937, at Monticello, Arkansas.[41]

James Mullins refused to stay out of trouble. After the Eastham Raid, he was arrested and given a jail term at Waxahachie, Texas, for harboring and aiding. After his jail term, he worked for officers in and around Dallas for federal investigators as a paid informer.[42] What he did to get money in January 1938 fit perfectly in Mullins' way of doing things. He took a small bottle of turpentine, walked up to the cashier at a business in Dallas, and threatened the cashier with the bottle, saying that it was a bottle of nitroglycerin. He then told the cashier to give him all the money, a total of $68. Since it worked, he went to another small business and tried the same ruse again. The second cashier didn't fall for the stunt, and instead she and others in the store followed Mullins into the street, calling out for help. In a short amount of time, a large crowd gathered and chased Mullins down the street. He kept the crowd at a distance by threatening them with the supposed bottle of nitroglycerin, but the crowd continued to follow him. He was caught by running into a policeman, who grabbed him and placed him under arrest.[43] This stunt cost the stool pigeon two twenty-five-year concurrent terms back in prison for robbery. Mullins was sent to the Wynne Farm and led a mutiny because he was replaced as a commissary clerk in 1943. The result was a 144-hour solitary lockup for him. That isn't the end of James Mullins, however. There is a record for him being sentenced on January 21, 1954, to seven and a half to fifteen years for armed robbery. No more is known of Mullins. He went to prison in 1954 using the alias of James Muller.[44]

On May 25, while Clyde Barrow was being lowered into a West Dallas grave, Raymond Hamilton arrived in Huntsville after receiving a ninety-nine-year sentence in Denton. For three days he worked in the Walls Unit at the woodpile. On May 28 a Walker County grand jury handed down a capital offense indictment as a habitual criminal against Hamilton and a trial date was sent on June 12, 1934. The state would seek the death penalty. Ray didn't have much chance after James Mullins cut a deal with the authorities that he would testify against Hamilton's involvement in Major Crowson's murder on condition his charges were dropped. To make it worse, witnesses to the murder of John N. Bucher also got on the stand against the outlaw, and affidavits of Hamilton's conviction in the Carmen State Bank robbery were another nail in his coffin. The jury reached its decision after sundown, and the shackled twenty-one-year-old who had caused so much havoc was brought into the courtroom.[45] The jury arrived next, Judge Dean not long after that.

"Have you reached a verdict?" Dean asked the foreman.

"Yes, we have your honor," was the answer. "We find the defendant, Raymond Hamilton, guilty. We hereby affix a penalty of death in the electric chair."[46]

On June 14, just two days after Ray Hamilton was sentenced to death, Joe Palmer was having his own problems. At 9:30 A.M. he was walking down a street in Davenport, Iowa. He was having one of his spells and his suit was in terrible need of a cleaning. Something he did still have in his possession were two Colt .45s that Clyde Barrow had given him right before the Sac City, Iowa, robbery.[47] Sometimes it doesn't pay to try and help people, and patrolman Elmer Schleuter found that out the hard way when he approached the disheveled man, who was trying to walk down the street despite great physical discomfort. All Joe Palmer needed to know was that a cop was coming his way, and without hesitation he pulled both pistols. Al Schultze, someone who drove up to help in the situation, ended up helping Palmer's flight from Iowa. Everyone got in the car for a ride.[48]

Fifteen miles west of town, however, Palmer started complaining about the way Schultze's car performed. Spotting another car, he sped up, overtaking Dr. W. H. Finch. The doctor's vehicle was a small coupe. Only three people could fit in the cab; Palmer, exhibiting his disdain for all lawmen, locked Officer Schleuter in the cramped rumble seat.[49]

"Move over," Palmer ordered. The doctor moved. At 3:30 A.M. on June 15, Palmer drove into St. Joseph, Missouri. Stopping the car, he turned to his captives. "I'll leave the car with y'all if you promise to turn around and head back to Iowa," Joe said, stuffing his pistols in his belt. Palmer then exited the car and started walking peacefully down the street, as if nothing had happened.[50]

Retrieving Schleuter from his cramped confines, Finch and Schultze drove straight to the headquarters of the St. Joseph police. Minutes later, a squad car full of officers located the unkempt kidnapper wandering along the same street where Finch, Schultze, and Schleuter had last seen him. The Texas outlaw offered no resistance as the cuffs were applied to his wrists.[51]

At first, the St. Joseph authorities were unaware of their prisoner's identity. However, a check of his fingerprints soon revealed Palmer's lengthy record. He was immediately transferred to Texas, where Lee Simmons waited.[52]

The killing of Crowson in the Eastham Farm break had occurred in Houston County, but District Attorney Max Rogers thought it doubtful that the state could get a fair trial there. So Rogers and Simmons asked for and obtained a change of venue by order of the district judge. The cases were transferred to Walker County, where Hamilton was tried and given the death penalty.[53]

Hamilton's trial got a great deal of play in the newspapers, and Judge S. W. Dean therefore granted a change of venue in Palmer's case from Walker to Grimes County, both counties in the Twelfth Judicial District under Judge Dean. Palmer also received the death penalty.[54]

Joe Palmer fought to escape the electric chair at Anderson on June 28 as he sought to refute the dying statement of Major Crowson. Palmer's court-appointed attorneys, H. L. Lewis Jr. of Anderson and Robert Smither of Huntsville, said they expected to call only three or four witnesses and that Palmer would not take the stand. He was being tried as a habitual criminal. Joe was assessed the death penalty on Friday, June 29, 1934, by a jury in Anderson that convicted him of the murder of Major Crowson. The jury deliberated for only twenty minutes. Palmer, who had frequently predicted that the extreme penalty would be imposed, forced a smile as the verdict was read. When sentence was pronounced, Palmer said, "I can go to the chair at Huntsville. It won't bother me at all. I had far rather die in the electric chair than spend four and a half years more in that prison, the most damnable place on earth."[55] According to Bud Russell, Chief Transfer Agent of the Texas Prison System, there was more to the statement as he watched from the courtroom. Russell was known across the nation as the last person to be messed with when it came to transferring prisoners. In an author's interview with his great-grandson, Robert H. Russell, on August 24, 1999, Robert described some events in the famous transfer agents' involvement in this case. "Uncle Bud" is what Bud Russell was called by everyone in the system.

"Get ready to move out, that's what Uncle Bud said," Bob began his story:

> That's what he told Joe Palmer and the others when he went to get him from Kentucky. The prisoners were instructed to "spread eagle" for a weapons search before the group left for Texas. Joe Palmer had known both Uncle Bud and his son Roy Russell for over thirteen years. He felt that cold steel of a neck shackle many times. As for going back to the Death House, Palmer had every intention to fight extradition. He knew what happened to his friends Bonnie Parker and Clyde Barrow, and it was Palmer's concern that Lee Simmons would send Frank Hamer to bring him back to Texas for execution. But really, Joe was concerned about not making the trip back to Texas. Simmons was the mastermind in tracking Bonnie and Clyde, so maybe with the Death House Escape and the Eastham Raid,

Joe would deserve a bullet as he "escaped" from the ex–Texas Ranger. It was only when Palmer learned that the Russells were going to escort him back to Huntsville that extradition was approved by Joe Palmer.

Bud Russell tells what happened after the jury returned for the verdict and sentence:

> I was just finishing lunch when the bailiff told me to return Palmer to the courtroom to hear the jury's verdict. Late in reaching the jail, I learned that Colonel Simmons had personally conducted Palmer before the Judge. Hastening to the courtroom, I reached the door just as the verdict was being read to Joe: "We, the jury, find the defendant guilty of murder as charged and assess his punishment at Death."

Palmer leaned forward, resting his hands on the counsel table and asking the court for permission to speak, which request was granted. Seemingly assured that the court would understand the message he wished to convey, choosing his words deliberately and speaking them clearly and crisply with fervor, he began:

> Judge, I would like for you to know that you have not taken anything from me. In the beginning I was willing to risk any and everything, even my own life, to be freed from that awful hole I was in. That farm is the most disgraceful place in Texas. It stinks in every citizen's nostrils. To all of you who are rejoicing over the prospects of my death, I will make this promise: I WILL MEET YOU AT THE PORTALS OF HELL. THE HOT SEAT HOLDS NO TERROR FOR ME![56]

So on June 29, a Walker County jury convicted Joe Palmer of the murder of Major Crowson. He was sentenced to death and removed to the Death House.[57] Raymond Hamilton jumped to his feet when he saw Palmer being led past his cell.[58]

"Well?" Ray inquired. "What is it?"

"I got 'the hot squat,'" Joe said, laughing.

Max Rogers was the prosecuting attorney for the State during both the Hamilton and Palmer trials. He doesn't remember much about the trials now, but there are strange aspects of the situation that he does remember. Later Judge Rogers, he recalls:

> Let's see, in 1934, I was about thirty years old. Roughly. Well, I was threatened a lot. I took a lot of care how I traveled, where I went, and never went anywhere by myself and things like that. Friends of Hamilton's, from Dallas. They'd tell people. I never gave it much thought, I just tried to take the best care of myself that I could. Not to be by myself. You see, Palmer and Hamilton were together, it didn't actually matter who pulled the trigger. There was no doubt we would get the death penalty. Those was rough days back then. There was so many bank robberies, we were being pushed by the press and the knowledgeable people and everything to get the cases to trial. Stop bank robbers.[59]

A prison dorm with the community wash, Christmas Day, 1944.
— Courtesy Hugh Kennedy

A field boss.
Note the length
of the gun barrel.
— Courtesy Hugh Kennedy

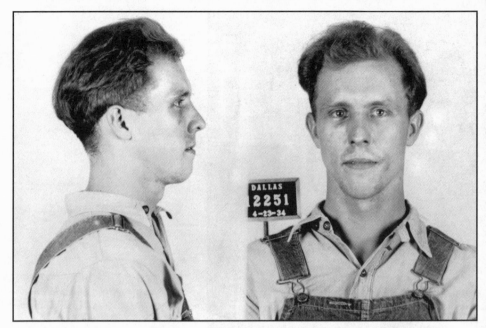

Mug shot of Floyd Hamilton. He would later be Public Enemy Number One.
— From the collection of the Texas/Dallas History
and Archives Division, Dallas Public Library

*Bonnie Parker
and Clyde Barrow
next to a B-400 Ford.*
— Courtesy Sandy Jones
Collection, John
Dillinger Society

Old Eastham viewed from the fields.
—Courtesy Texas Dept. of Criminal Justice

Old Eastham as a fully functional prison facility.
—Courtesy Texas Dept. of Criminal Justice

*Photo taken by Hugh Kennedy near the site of the Eastham Raid in 1934.
This was taken within two months of the actual raid.*
— Courtesy Hugh Kennedy

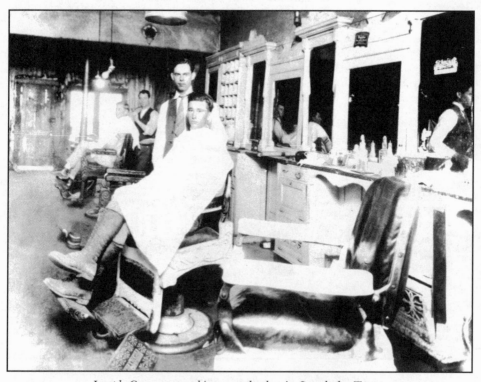

*Joseph Crowson working as a barber in Lovelady, Texas,
before he was hired at Eastham State Farm.*
— Courtesy Marc Crowson

Major Crowson as a highrider, or long-arm man, at Eastham.
— Courtesy Marc Crowson

The bridge Bonnie Parker was parked near at the Calhoun Ferry Road.

Underpinnings of the same bridge. Clyde Barrow and James Mullins hid in the creek with BARs until the shooting started.

Major Crowson's grave in Lovelady, Texas.

Rare photo of Clyde Barrow with a pair of .45 pistols and Joe Palmer with Clyde's whippit shotgun. The car is a 1934 Pontiac.
— Courtesy Sandy Jones Collection, John Dillinger Society

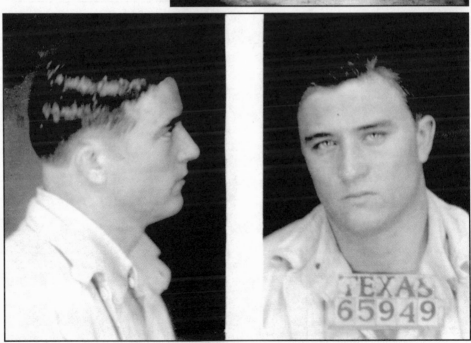

Mug shot of Henry Methvin.
—From the collection of the Texas/Dallas History and Archives Division, Dallas Public Library

*Photo of Thula and
Whitey Walker in Florida
shortly before the bank
ambush.*
— Courtesy Sandra Walker

*Whitey Walker in Florida
with a 1934 Ford,
probably taken near the
beach. Possibly the last photo
ever taken of Whitey before
the shotgun blast.*
— Courtesy Janet Johnson

Looking down the corridor in the Death House. During the escape, the stairs were not there and the showers behind them stood the green door. To the right of the photo was the Death House entrance that Charlie Frazier entered.

Mug shot of Charlie Frazier.
— Courtesy Texas Prison Archives, Criminal Justice, Institutional Division, TDCJ-1D

Walls Unit in Huntsville as it would have appeared during the Death House Escape.
—Courtesy Texas Dept. of Criminal Justice

Overview of the Walls Unit, taken from a catwalk on a wall. In the photo we
are looking toward picket 7.
—Courtesy Texas Dept. of Criminal Justice

Aerial view of Walls prison. Note the corner pickets that form a "Z" shape. Contrary to claims made in other publications, this is the wall at which the Death House Escape actually occurred.

—Courtesy Texas Dept. of Criminal Justice

*Grave of
William Jennings
Bryan Walker
in the family plot.*

*The
electric chair.*
— Courtesy Jim
Willett

Gravestone of Joe Palmer in San Antonio.

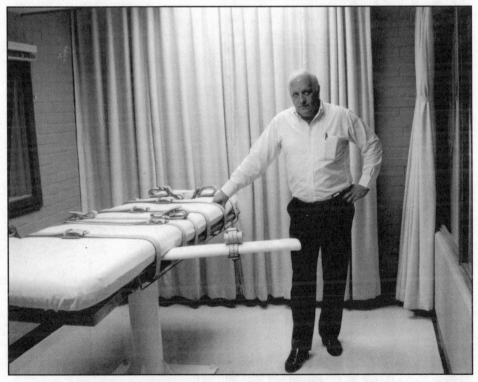

Warden Jim Willett against the gurney in the execution chamber.

Sometimes called the final death row. The cells are not numbered. The artificial flowers lend a macabre touch.

The end row cell where the condemned spends most of his time before the execution.

Walking toward the final light.
When a condemned prisoner sees this view,
there is no turning back, and there are
no more appeals or stays of execution.

CHAPTER 12

Busted in Florida:
The Beginning of the End

I t is almost comical the way that the Whitey Walker Gang continued to escape apprehension. The gang just looked a target over, did what they had planned to do for the most part, and then left for another target. As the Barrow Gang was being shot to pieces (and returning the favor), the Whitey Walker Gang drove in the night to their next destination.

That is why it is so disturbing that the gang would be busted for something so stupid. Maybe there was no other way to accomplish what they wanted. Maybe they were tired. Maybe there wasn't a "they" and only one member screwed up. Either way, the gang was about to be broken up—in a way, they already had. Blackie Thompson had separated from the other members of the gang. Whitey Walker and the mysterious Roy Johnson, who was charged in all the armed robberies but only seen at the Caldwell Jewelry Store robbery, were in Tallahassee, Florida.

Three days after the disappearance of the gang, Falls County authorities investigating the First State Bank of Marlin robbery and the kidnapping of the employees tried to trace a mud-spattered car seen at 10:00 A.M. at North Zulch, a little town ten miles west of Madisonville.[1]

The car was occupied by two men said to resemble Whitey Walker and Blackie Thompson. In the meantime, the grand jury

121

convened on December 30 in Marlin to continue the inquiry about the robbery.[2]

A break came in late January of 1934 when a suspect was reported held in Miami, Florida, pending an investigation in connection with the robbery of the First State Bank of Marlin. Something big was going on in the Sunshine State. Sheriff M. M. Reese of Falls County directed an inquiry to the chief of police in Miami for circumstances surrounding the detention of a man they were holding. A man had been arrested outside a tavern in the city. Reese wanted to know further details about the man to determine if he could be connected with the Marlin robbery.[3] In his message to the Florida authorities, the sheriff advised them that Walker, Thompson, and Johnson were sought for questioning in connection with the robbery, and their fingerprints were forwarded to Miami. A description of the loot stolen in the robbery of the Marlin bank was also forwarded for comparison with money reported found on the man being held.

The reason sheriff Reese was so interested in this man was due to a report that the suspect was picked up there after displaying a sum of money estimated at about $5,000. That in itself was only a bit unusual. Suspicion arose, however, when he paid $1,500 cash in full for a Cadillac automobile, and he paid for the car in denominations of $5, $10, and $20 bills. The clincher was that some of the $100 bills in his possession were issued by Waco and Marlin banks. He was also said to have had 848 $1 bills and a quantity of dimes. It would soon be learned that he was also armed with an automatic pistol during his arrest, but he had not resisted. There was also talk that the man had been seen with a companion who also had a large amount of money.[4]

A dispatch received by a local newspaper, *The Marlin Daily Democrat,* filed in Miami at 2:30 P.M. Monday, January 29,[5] said a suit had been filed by the held man, a Mr. Howard Peoples, in circuit court for recovery of money said to have been found in his possession when he was taken into custody. This was probably not a very wise move, because once arrested, Peoples was fingerprinted, and through that identification it became obvious that the name Howard Peoples was a spur-of-the-moment alias for Irvin "Blackie" Thompson.[6]

According to a report to the Falls County Sheriff's office, Thompson had $5,400 in his car and a big wad of bills in his pocket. A press report also said there was $5,700 to Peoples' credit in a Florida bank.[7]

The same day of the press report on the Peoples/Thompson money issue, the rest of the gang were having a hard time of it. In Tallahassee, Florida, someone had tipped off police of an intended robbery of one of the big banks where a large sum of state money was deposited. Several policeman watched the Capital City Bank from both the inside and outside. True to the tip, two of the robbers appeared at an early hour. Officers from the outside called officers inside the bank, and the two squads closed in on the robbers, who fled, still in their car. Officers shot out the rear tires, slowing the fugitives down. An officer went around toward the front of the fleeing vehicle just in time to fire a round of buckshot into Whitey Walker, shattering his arm and causing minor damage to Roy Johnson's arm as well.[8] Whitey Walker and Roy Johnson were taken into the custody of Sheriff Stoutmire in Tallahassee, Florida.[9]

In Marlin, Texas, a second message was received by Sheriff Reese that afternoon. The message was from the Tallahassee sheriff and read, "Homer Arthur, Mrs. Walker, and another woman are in jail here," in addition to Walker and Johnson. Sheriff Reese had no information regarding the party referred to as "Arthur." Walker was described in the message as "shot with two buckshot in his arm." The message to Sheriff Reese continued to read that a considerable amount of diamonds and other jewelry, as well as $14,000 in cash and bonds, were recovered. The value of the diamonds and jewelry had not been checked. In addition, the message said the Florida authorities recovered six pistols, one pump shotgun, two high-powered rifles, two sawed-off shotguns, one Ford coupe, and one Ford sedan and coach. Money taken from the bandits, and the description of the money deposited by them in certain banks, largely consisted of $20, $10, $5, and $1 bills, some bills being issued by the First National of Waco. This led to a check with Waco and Marlin. Later a canvas money bag marked, "First State Bank, Marlin, Texas" was recovered from the bandit's apartment.

In letters found by authorities, six Florida banks were marked as robbery targets. The banks, he said, were the Lewis State and Capital City in Tallahassee; the Farmers and Mer-

chants in Monticello, Florida; First National Bank in Coral
Gables; Little River Bank and Trust Company in Miami; and
First Hollywood Bank in Hollywood. Each of the banks held
deposits that had been made by one of the three men. Through
these deposits, the bandits could visit the institutions at closing
time as depositors without creating suspicion.

The gang had rented a house in Miami, had one of their
new automobiles adjusted to go more than one hundred miles
an hour, and had tentatively selected a farm outside Tallahassee
as a hideout. Blackie Thompson was supposed to join Walker
and Johnson in Tallahassee on the morning of the proposed
robbery, but he was sitting in a Miami jail cell.[10]

In Anderson County, Texas, authorities instituted steps to
obtain extradition papers from the governor of Texas for return
of the gang for the robbery of the Palestine bank. The three
men and Walker's wife were under indictment for the robbery.
The cooperation of Brazos and Milam County authorities had
also been arranged in a joint effort to bring the men back in
connection with the Buckholts and Bryan robberies, while a
request had been made of Florida authorities to hold Walker's
wife. The arrangement agreed upon, including Falls County for
the Marlin bank robbery, was that an officer from the Anderson
County sheriff's office at Palestine would be sent to Florida for
the prisoners. While that was being arranged, Attorney George
Carter, representing the First State Bank of Marlin, left that
Monday night for Florida. He carried the serial numbers of certain securities taken from the bank. A Florida report stated that
a quantity of bonds were found in possession of members of the
gang when arrested on Monday in Tallahassee.[11]

The Walker Gang was run down in Florida largely through
the work of Norman J. York, the manager of the Burn Agency
in Houston. He was instrumental in their identification in connection with the Caldwell Jewelry robbery and kidnapping in
Bryan and spent about two weeks working on the Marlin bank
case. He also had much to do with the indictment of all three by
a Falls County grand jury.[12]

To make matters worse on the personal side of things, Roy
Johnson had taken a wife. Disillusioned by the arrest of her husband, his bride of two weeks returned to her home in Texas with

her parents. They had driven all the way to Florida to get her. The poor woman didn't even know who Roy was; she thought her husband was Bob Allen, a baseball player, not an escaped Oklahoma convict sought in connection with robberies in Texas. Giving him a last goodbye kiss through the bars of a jail cell, she was quoted as saying, "I'll always love him. He was sweet to me. Too sweet. I guess I'm spoiled." She added, "Now that it's all happened, I'm glad I found out about Bob as soon as I did. It would have been much harder to part if we had been married longer." Johnson was quoted as telling the girl to "go back to Texas and have the marriage annulled." He also commented, "Next time I get out, there'll be so many dogs behind me I won't have time to stop and see you."[13]

Rewards of $100 each had been arranged from Falls, Milam, Brazos, and Anderson Counties, making a total of $400 available, with the understanding that Walker, his wife, Johnson, and Thompson would be returned to Texas. The Walkers and Johnson were placed in the Anderson County jail in Palestine on Sunday. It was feared that Walker might lose the arm hit by buckshot, the wounds being so bad that amputation was considered an option.[14]

Oklahoma officers delivered Blackie Thompson to Sheriff Boyd of Palestine and Deputy E. W. Willoughby of Gregg County at Gladewater. $20,000 in cash, $14,300 in bonds, three automobiles, and a quantity of jewelry found in possession of Blackie Thompson, Whitey Walker, and Roy Johnson were tied up by court orders obtained in Florida on the petition of Attorney George H. Carter.

Lee Humphrey, the bank janitor who was taken for a ride by the bandits the day the Marlin bank was robbed, recognized Thompson in the Palestine jail, and Walker by George Davis, a janitor of a Marlin drugstore. The two men were taken to Palestine by Sheriff Reese for that purpose. Davis had seen one of the men at the drugstore a short time before the bank was robbed. Walker was going to make the best of a bad situation while in the media spotlight. With his right arm still wrapped in bandages, the hand extending toward the ceiling of his cell in the Anderson County jail in Palestine, he said with emphasis that the Tallahassee officer who shot him was entirely too easy on the trigger.

"I am not afraid of brave men," he said. "But it's the other kind that will shoot you when you least expect it, and one of these St. Vitus deputies is just as apt to shoot his best friend as anyone else. I have known a lot of them, too," he added while holding his wounded right arm. His wife was held in the same cell as her husband, and that story would get stranger and more complicated as to *which* Mrs. Whitey Walker authorities actually wanted, Dolores or Thula. The outlaw was bitter about being shot, saying he wasn't resisting arrest when he was hit with the shotgun blast. How could he reach for his gun and hold his hands up at the same time?

"I couldn't reach the ignition and hold both hands up at the same time, and after I was shot, the St. Vitus deputy was all the time punching me in the face with the muzzle of his gun threatening to shoot me again if I didn't stick 'em up. I stuck up my left arm, but my right was so nearly shot off I couldn't stick it up."

Thula sat in silence on her bunk while Whitey was talking, and short of a few questions by the police, Walker stole the show, seeming to be almost relieved that he could tell stories to an audience. Just around the corner in another cell, Thompson and Roy Johnson were being held, and they also appeared to enjoy so much conversation and so many visitors, even to the point of dressing their best for the early Sunday afternoon callers. The removal of the prisoners from the Anderson County jail was generally agreed upon by officers of the several counties that now had a proprietary claim on them in separate jails, so that "If one should get out, we still have the rest of them," as Sheriff Boyd explained it.[15]

The state asked for the death penalty for Whitey Walker, Blackie Thompson, and Roy Johnson after a Brazos County grand jury indicted them for robbery with firearms in connection with the December 16 robbery of the Caldwell Jewelry Store, as well as the kidnapping of the Caldwells in Bryan. Warrants were issued for the three men and sent to Palestine, where Walker and his wife were held in jail, and others were sent to Harris County where Thompson and Johnson were recently transferred from Palestine.[16]

The cases of Whitey Walker, Blackie Thompson, and R. A. Johnson, charged with robbery of the Caldwell Jewelry Store in Bryan, were docketed to be called up in Brazos County district court Wednesday, March 7, 1934. The trio were also indicted in connection with the robbery of the First State Bank of Marlin. Marlin was anxious to get its hands on the Fishing Hole Gang as well, and the local authorities indicated an intention to assign the cases in Marlin at the earliest possible date. That way Falls County would get them as soon as the Bryan trial was finished.[17]

Thompson, whose trial has been assigned on the Falls County district court docket for Monday, March 12, was taken to Bryan from Marlin, while six deputy sheriffs took Walker from Palestine to Bryan. It was obvious that the law was not taking any chances on an escape by the leader of the gang, even with an arm shot to pieces. A physician's certificate had shown that Walker was ill when the Falls County sheriff went to Palestine to get him that Saturday. Thompson was moved to Marlin from Houston, where he and Johnson had been held in the Harris County jail, and that is how the musical chairs went before anyone went to trial in Bryan. Eventually, all of the defendants ended up in Bryan for the Caldwell Jewelry heist.

Thula Hunt Walker, Whitey's current wife, was returned to Palestine. However, at this point some information had come to light that made the situation more confusing. A woman known as Dolores Walker, Whitey's former wife, had been indicted in connection with the bank robbery in Palestine.[18]

The three men had been lodged in separate cells in the Brazos County jail and were guarded day and night. Extra lights had been strung about the jail as an added precaution.[19] Some people recalled that there was a machine gun nest on the roof of the courthouse in case Bonnie and Clyde tried to rescue their friends like in the Eastham Raid.

Most of the jurymen who were disqualified admitted they had discussed the case and had formed an opinion. There were some others who were disqualified because they did not believe in the death penalty. County Attorney Oak McKenzie, assisted by F. L. Henderson and S. C. Hoyle Jr., was prosecuting the case, and J. G. Minkert represented all three defendants. All the lawyers made it clear that the selection of the jury probably would be a long, drawn-out affair.

At the convening of court after the noon recess, Attorney Minkert filed a motion for a continuance, based upon the absence of witnesses that he contended to be important to the defense. The motion was overruled by Judge W. C. Davis, and the defendants were ordered into court and the venire called. The defense attorney then tried another tactic by making a motion at the opening of the morning session for a different continuance. The grounds were that Walker was not physically able to remain in court for the trial. Drs. R. B. Ehlinger and John W. Black were called to make an examination, and in their opinion Walker was able to stand the physical strain. When court opened that morning, the room was crowded, with every available seat taken. Several scores of men and women crowded the corridors downstairs and stood about the west door of the courthouse. The crowd included a few women, which was unique for that time period. People sitting in the back of the courtroom couldn't hear any testimony, but no one was going to miss the trial if they could squeeze themselves in through the doors.

Special deputies, a much greater number than had been on duty in the Brazos district court in the past, were there, all heavily armed. Walker gave evidence of the effect of his injury as he appeared pale and moved slowly. His right arm was in a splint, and he carried it at a right angle from his body, supporting it with his left hand. Several people had recognized pictures of Walker and Thompson as the men in the robbery.[20]

Thompson was scheduled to go to trial in Falls County district court Monday on an indictment returned against him, along with Walker and Johnson, in connection with the robbery of the First State Bank in Marlin. Judge E. M. Dodson announced the appointments of a Mr. Patterson and Mr. Reagan, Marlin attorneys, to represent the defendant.[21] Why Blackie was selected to be tried separately in Marlin and selected to be the first tried is unknown. It would prove to be the worst situation that could have happened to him.

The trial in Bryan lasted four days from the time of jury selection to the final verdict. John Sealy Caldwell told a story of rough and brutal treatment of himself and his wife, including threats of permanent maiming and death from Whitey Walker, Blackie Thompson, and Roy Johnson.[22] The courtroom was crowded throughout the day, and the excitement paralleled the atmosphere at a circus. Deputies were on guard in the corridors and at the one stairway that was open to the courtroom. Hundreds of men and women were turned away for lack of room. The defense called witnesses in an effort to prove an alibi for both Walker and Johnson. These witnesses were Everett Cole of Rogers, where Walker lived, and R. L. Brown, a fisherman from Ida, Louisiana, with whom Johnson is said to have spent some time in November, December, and January, finally leaving there, according to Brown, for Florida on a honeymoon trip.

The state called several witnesses to refute the testimony. Among them were T. M. Jameson, an Arkansas game warden, and O. H. Harris, a federal game warden, both of DeWitt, Arkansas, and Mr. and Mrs. E. F. Parks of Bryan, from whom it is said the Walker Gang rented a house December 1, living in it until the night of December 14, the date of the robbery, or early the next morning.

Cole stated that he had known Walker for a number of years and that he saw him about sundown on the night of December 14 at the home of Walker's father. He said it was the first time he had seen Whitey in about four years and that he talked with him for a short time. A cross examination that he saw Walker on the night of the robbery did not change the testimony at all.

When R. L. Brown got on the stand, he stated that he operated a fishing camp near Ida and that each Friday he peddled fish in that vicinity. He told the jury that he first saw Johnson, whom he said went under the name of Robert Allen, sometime after November 15 and that he went hunting with him. The next time he saw him was December 15 or 16, when Johnson, alias Allen, came to his camp between sundown and 11:00 that night. He didn't seem sure of the date but said he thought the day of the week was Thursday, as the next day was Friday, his fish peddling day. He didn't peddle fish that day because he was with Johnson, and Ida was three hundred miles away from Bryan. Brown continued by saying that he and Johnson went to Arkansas on a hunting trip on December 19, and he had bought a car from Johnson. Roy had told him he had bought the car in Kil-

gore, but gave the name of A. R. Gregory at the time of pur-
chase. Brown then said he later sold the car back to Johnson. On
January 18 Roy went to Florida on a honeymoon, and he knew
the woman Johnson married. After the Arkansas trip, he said
Johnson came to Ida, accompanied by a man whose name was
given as Homer Arthur, and also Arthur's sister. Brown identified a picture of Arthur given to him by County Attorney Oak
McKenzie. The car that Johnson had was described by Brown as
a two-door sedan, painted gray. John Sealy Caldwell was then
recalled to the stand and testified that the car used by the robbers was a dark four-door sedan.

E. F. Parks of Bryan was then called to the stand by the
state. He identified Walker and Thompson as the two men he
saw at the house that had been rented by Walker from Mrs.
Parks on December 1, 1933. Mrs. Parks had told him she had
been told the renters wanted to buy a garage. Hearing of one for
sale, Mr. Parks said he went to the house to tell the men, and
that at that time he saw Walker and Thompson. He was positive
in his identification.

Mrs. E. F. Parks was then called by the state. She said that
on the night of December 1, a woman came to her home to see
about renting the Parks' rent house on Baker Avenue. She went
to show the house and that Walker, who went by the name of Joe
E. Parks, was the man who went through the house with her. She
said the house was dark and that Walker used a flashlight. In
identifying Walker, she asked if he had gold in his teeth, and it
was found that he did. Mrs. Parks said that Walker and his party
had three automobiles, a coupe, a two-door sedan, and a four-
door sedan, all Fords and all dark in color.[23]

Arguments closed, and the jury was sent out to deliberate
the fate of these men. The jury, which began deliberating about
4:00 Saturday afternoon reported at about 10:00 Sunday morning that it had arrived at a verdict. At 11:00 A.M., the jurors filed
into the courtroom to make their report to Judge W. C. Davis.
J. L. Powers was the foreman. Sentences of ninety-nine years
each were given to J. W. "Whitey" Walker, Irvin "Blackie"
Thompson, and Roy Johnson, found guilty of robbery of the
Caldwell Jewelry Store with firearms. After reading the verdict,
Judge Davis stated that the prisoners could not be sentenced on

Sunday. He said that if the defense waived the two days allowed in which to file a motion for a new trial, he would sentence the three men Monday morning. He also left instructions for someone to get in touch with sheriff M. M. Reese of Marlin to advise him to come for the prisoners on Monday. Judge Davis announced that he would formally sentence Walker and Johnson Wednesday morning. After that, they would be taken to Huntsville to serve their sentence.

Thompson was taken to Marlin by Sheriff Reese and some deputies. He would be put on trial at once for that bank robbery, for which the three men were indicted separately. If Falls County authorities were through with Thompson by Wednesday, he would be brought back to Bryan for sentencing at the same time as Walker and Johnson. The three defendants took the sentence of life in prison calmly Sunday morning. After the verdict had been read by Judge Davis, Walker spoke to Thompson and grinned, and Thompson nodded his head and grinned back. The death penalty was the only verdict feared.

On the first ballot, six of the jurors were for death, five for ninety-nine years, and one for fifty years. During the night and the next morning, other ballots were taken. Two jurors refused to vote the death penalty and practically forced the verdict that was returned. As the jury continued its deliberations, the spirits of the defendants rose, and one guard reported that Johnson offered to bet his "$100 watch" against $15 of Thompson's cash that "we don't get the hot seat."

The news that the jury had reached a verdict spread rapidly, and the courtroom was filled by the time Judge Davis appeared. Many in the audience were cadets from Allen Academy, a local military school.[24]

Thompson jumped from one trial to a new one the next day. Since he was convicted, he could technically be sent on to Marlin for the bank robbery and kidnapping charges there, and he was. However, he would have to come back to Bryan for formal sentencing. After several failed motions by Thompson's defense, the trial in Marlin got underway. C. M. Pearce, district attorney, indicated he would ask for the death penalty for Thompson.[25] Arguments were opened by R. D. Peterson, the assistant district attorney for the state, followed by lawyers Reagan and Patterson for the defense, and C. M. Pearce, the district attorney.[26]

Thompson took an interest in all the proceedings, and during jury selection he smoked an occasional cigarette until the practice was banned for everyone except attorneys. This was because of the large crowd and closed windows. The trial testimony was nearly completed late Wednesday, March 15, of Blackie's role in the $41,000 robbery of the First State Bank. Two witnesses identified Thompson as one of two men who robbed the bank and who threatened to put out their eyes if they didn't keep them closed. The state completed its rebuttal, and the defense had offered all its evidence except the testimony from witnesses due on Thursday. These witnesses were intended to prove Thompson was in Amarillo at the time of the robbery. Witnesses summoned by the defense were C. W. Culwell, an Amarillo attorney, Miss Joie Jones of Houston, and Miss Viola Simmons of Fort Worth.[27]

Following state testimony regarding the reputation for truth and veracity of Mrs. Tillie Mae Stanley, who had previously been called by the defendant, the defense placed Bill Bowlin, an Amarillo service station operator, on the stand to testify on this point. Mrs. Stanley had testified that she was with Thompson in Amarillo until after midnight a few hours before the early morning of December 27, when bank employees alleged that Thompson took part in the robbery. The state offered a witness who testified it took him a day to drive a car from Amarillo to Marlin.[28] Following Thursday's testimony, attorneys for both sides made their final arguments and the case was given to the jury.

Back in Bryan, Walker and Johnson were taken to the state prison on Wednesday immediately after sentence was passed by Judge W. C. Davis.[29] Since Thompson was still on trial in Marlin on Wednesday, he was not sentenced with his two pals.

Death was the sentence for Irvin "Blackie" Thompson. The verdict was returned by the jury at 1:35 Thursday afternoon, finding him guilty of an indictment charging robbery with firearms in connection with the holdup December 27 of the First State Bank of Marlin and kidnapping three employees. The jury was polled individually at the request of Thompson's lawyer, and after each had indicated that was his verdict, the defendant was handcuffed to a deputy sheriff and taken back to jail.

The defense planned and gave notice of an appeal to the Texas Court of Criminal Appeals in Austin, and they had good reason. There appeared to be some monkey business going on after the jury retired to deliberate. The usual generic reasons were listed in Thompson's appeal, but the conduct of the jury was a very real concern, as it pertained to a death sentence.

In connection with the conduct allegations, four members of the jury were called to testify. Charlie Schmidt of Rosebud, a member of the jury, had stated that while they were deliberating, the question came up of whether the defendant would have to serve a life term given to him in Bryan before being executed under a death penalty in the Marlin court. Someone suggested that the court be asked about it, but it was decided to strike that out and not consider it. Schmidt said he had read of the Bryan sentence and also of Thompson's escape from an Oklahoma prison, but he did not hear the latter mentioned by any members of the jury. On cross examination, he said his verdict was based on the evidence offered in the case on trial. Under re-direct examination, he said that when he was being examined as a venire men, and that the defense counsel did not ask him if he knew about Thompson's previous record.

Similar testimony was given by three other members of the jury: F. H. Lampert, Ed Phillips, and J. H. Douglas.

At the afternoon session of court, the state called the other eight members of the jury for questioning in regards to whether the reference to the life term was made before or after final vote for the death penalty.[30]

The following is from the court transcript:

F. H. Lambert,
    A witness for the defendant, after having been duly sworn, testified:
Direct Examination
By Mr. Patterson:
    My name is F. H. Lambert; I was a juror in the case of the State of Texas v. Irvin Thompson, tried on the week of March 12th. Yes sir, I remember the Wednesday afternoon while I was on the jury when the Judge recessed the case about two

o'clock until next morning; that was on Wednesday. After we retired that evening, I guess some of them were playing dominoes and some shaving, I couldn't tell whether they were that evening or not. I don't remember a discussion of the defendant having been convicted down at Bryan and given 99 years in that case; I didn't hear it. I don't know whether or not it was brought up. I do not remember anyone discussing the fact that he had escaped from an Oklahoma penitentiary on that particular Wednesday afternoon, no sir. I heard that he had been convicted at Bryan the morning before I got here. Yes sir, before I was taken on the jury. I did not hear about him escaping from the Oklahoma penitentiary before I was taken on the jury. I do not remember his term down at Bryan being mentioned any time after we had gone into deliberation.

Yes sir, I remember a juror asking a question as to whether or not [the] defendant would have to be executed if given the death penalty or would have to serve 99 years first— I heard that. Yes sir, that was the morning we retired for deliberation, Thursday morning. No one discussed it before this particular question was asked. It was not mentioned before he asked the question, no sir, I don't think so. No sir, when that was mentioned, the jurors were not all around the table—that was mentioned about thirty minutes after we went in.

No sir, I do not remember one of the jurors popping up and making the statement "the defendant already has 216 years—more than he will ever serve"—I didn't hear that. No sir, I do not remember hearing a juror say that the defendant already had more time than he would ever serve, and we ought to give him a sentence that would stick. I couldn't tell you whether all the jurors knew about the defendant being convicted at Bryan.

Cross Examination

By Mr. Pearce:

Yes sir, I knew that he had been convicted or had seen newspaper reports prior to the time I was taken on the jury. Yes sir, someone in the jury room asked that if we gave him the death penalty whether he would have to serve 99 years or be electrocuted, and somebody spoke up and said we would have to write it on paper and ask the court about it, and that was about all the discussion. We made up the verdict from the evidence we heard in the trial of this case.[31]

In Huntsville, Thompson would be within the same walls that held Walker and Johnson. Prison authorities notified C. M. Pearce, the district attorney, that they planned to reset Walker's wounded arm.[32] On Saturday Thompson was placed in the death cell at the Texas Penitentiary in Huntsville. He was taken to Huntsville by Sheriff Reese and Deputies Pamplin and Hay after his motion for a new trial had been overruled by Judge Dodson in the Falls County district court. Thompson's lawyer gave notice of appeal. On the way to the penitentiary, the group stopped at Bryan, where Thompson was sentenced to serve ninety-nine years in prison on the conviction in connection with the robbery of the Caldwell Jewelry Store there. While in Huntsville, Sheriff Reese saw W. J. "Whitey" Walker under treatment in the penitentiary hospital. Johnson was also confined in the prison Walls Unit.[33] In a side note, Blackie Thompson's Amarillo alibi received her own bad news. An indictment was returned against Mrs. Tillie Mae Stanley, arrested by Amarillo officers with a charge of perjury because of her testimony at the Marlin trial.

The Marlin trial of Whitey Walker and Roy Johnson was for the most part a carbon copy of Thompson's earlier trial. There was one major exception. This Marlin jury let Walker and Johnson live. A verdict of guilty and an assessment of the defendant's punishment as ninety-nine years' confinement in the Texas penitentiary was returned by a jury in Falls County district court shortly after 9:00 Friday morning. Walker accepted the sentence Monday morning without appeal.

Walker, who was held in the Falls County Jail for two weeks, left immediately in the charge of Sheriff Reese for the penitentiary in Huntsville to begin serving term.[34]

So the entire gang was incarcerated in the Walls Unit in downtown Huntsville, Texas. Two gang members had life sentences, with yet another set of life sentences waiting for them in Oklahoma. The third member sat in a cell of row seven—the Death House. After an already long criminal life by seasoned outlaw standards, the story was still not finished. Blackie Thompson looked down the corridor of the Death House toward the electric chair called Ol' Sparky, hidden from its customers a few yards away but he would never sit in it. His friend and long-time business associate Whitey Walker would see to that. Even though his arm was severely damaged and he was in the prison hospital, Walker was not about to let his friend die in the chair. Walker had friends, and he made deadly associates. Roy Johnson was also there to help. The Fishing Hole Gang wasn't finished, it had just moved to a different place with a different motive. Besides, Charlie Frazier, the most notorious escape artist in the Southwest, was on their side. . . .

CHAPTER 13

Over the Wall

When the metal door to the old Death House is opened in the Walls Unit, the feelings of fear start slowly, way back in your mind, like touching a snake that isn't poisonous. There is nothing to fear, really, just an instinctive dread that cannot be shaken off—fought yes, but not completely forgotten.

The metal stairs leading down into the Death House corridor are steep, and when a person walks on them, the rail must be held to prevent falling. The silence is broken with the annoying creak of a hinge and the metallic grate as boots meet the metal steps. There is a dim light cascading down through one of the dust-coated windows on the wall of the corridor. The prison is built on a hill, and where a person is standing in relation to the ground level is often confusing. The walls are thick. So thick that the difference in temperature can be felt immediately when one walks down the stairs. Three or four light bulbs are still in line on the ceiling of the nine-cell structure that is the seventh row of the prison. A 1930 blueprint shows this area to be row fifteen, but no one can remember it being called anything but seven row. A single shower hides behind the base of the stairs of the forty-five-foot corridor. This shower was not here in 1934. Prisoners washed themselves in a bucket, and the dirty water was then poured down a drain across from cell two. The structure

137

was different in the summer of 1934. Where the shower is now there was a green door. The condemned prisoner in cell one was almost close enough to touch that door. On the far end of the corridor near cell eight was a barber's chair. That was for haircuts and a shave, but it was also for the preparation of a prisoner about to be electrocuted. There were no stairs. The stairs were added when the wing became part of the hospital on the grounds. The seventh row was a single story, unlike the threetier setup in the rest of the prison. There was a door leading directly to the courtyard toward the north end of the corridor. The door opening was bricked up years ago.

One cell, cell four, has added wire mesh on the front for a very special tenant. There is a bunk and sink for each prisoner sentenced to die, one prisoner per cell. Each cell must be locked and unlocked individually with a key. The electric chair waits nearby, sitting just twenty feet behind Death House cell number one. Past the green door of the Death House was a curtain, and behind the curtain was the chair, the chair that makes a person's blood boil in their body and smoke rise from the pores of their hands—the chair that switches from 1,800 volts to 500, up to 1,300, and back to 500 volts as its occupant "rides the lightning" for a full minute. The intervals are necessary so that the convict won't catch fire.[1] A covering goes over the eyes so the orbs do not disengage from their sockets.

The outside walls were shaped different. It wasn't a square red brick wall going all the way around like it is today; the back corners were shaped in a Z pattern, making the guard pickets in different places which included a blind spot. Where there is now a cement courtyard, there once was a full line of trees and foliage and all kinds of plants making it easy to hide.

On July 22, 1934, at 4:20 P.M., one of the most dramatic events in the history of the Texas Prison System started at the thick metal door leading into the Death House. This event became more than a security breach—it became a personal affront to Lee Simmons, the director of the Texas Prison System. Simmons already had taken matters into his own hands regarding the infamous Eastham Raid by Clyde Barrow in January of the same year. It was because of Simmons' intervention with Governor Miriam Ferguson that ex–Texas Ranger Frank Hamer took charge of the Barrow Gang chase throughout the Southwest.

Charlie Frazier, whose real name was Eldridge Roy Johnson, was well known in the Texas, Arkansas, and Louisiana penal systems for his stubbornness in escape attempts. Born near Waskom, Texas, in 1895, Frazier (as Texas records refer to him) tended to react to situations more than think about them. What he may have lacked in brains he made up for in sheer guts. This man would jump into any frying pan of trouble with both feet. His temper and his habit of playing a bad hand of poker seemed to always get the better of him. He was also the leader of a prison group called the Red Hat Gang. On September 10, 1933, Frazier and eleven other convicts escaped from Louisiana's Angola Prison, one of the most brutal and bloody prison escapes in the history of the state. This was just another day for the ringleader. According to Joe Bauske, a relative of Charlie, the man got his start in crime in 1916 when he and some friends stole ten cases of whiskey valued at ten dollars a case from the hamlet of Annona and drove the stash a few miles away to Clarksville, Texas, which was the group's hometown.[2] Whatever happened to him immediately after that is uncertain, but on January 13, 1917, he was convicted of bank robbery in Annona County and sent to the penitentiary at Huntsville.[3] On August 11 of that year, he took an unauthorized trip out of prison but was recaptured in two days. In January the following year Frazier escaped again, this time making it in hiding until July 24, when he was recaptured in Hugo, Oklahoma. His next chance was on October 10, 1918, and he was recaptured the same day.[4] In February 1920 he was discharged, but by June he had tacked on an eight- to ten-year term in Louisiana for robbery and burglary using the alias R. E. Johnson.

Paroled in July of 1922, Frazier lasted until November, when he was sent to Louisiana State Penitentiary for another burglary, this time using the alias A. W. Adams. Between December 4, 1925, and July 27, 1928, he escaped and was recaptured four more times, and while on the outside he managed to accrue an additional twenty-five years of prison time for robbery with firearms, burglary, and theft.[5] The December 26, 1927, escape enabled him to add a murder to his rap sheet in Arkansas. This crime gave him a life sentence in Arkansas, but the governor commuted his sentence to twenty-one years. Frazier entered the Arkansas State Penitentiary as #25872. Governor Parnell granted Charlie a fifteen-day furlough on December 23, 1932, exactly one year after his sentence was commuted. The favor was returned by his not returning to prison.[6] This gave Frazier time to commit an April 12, 1933, robbery and attempted murder in Benton, Louisiana. All told, he now had to his credit a life sentence, an eighteen- to twenty-eight-year additional sentence, and all the time he had yet to serve on his December 4, 1925, escape. Charlie Frazier was then sent to Angola to direct the most infamous event of his life. He made it long enough to try an East Texas robbery only to be arrested and sent to the Walls Unit in Huntsville as prisoner #76683.[7] That was fine with him, because Louisiana wasn't looking too kindly at Eldridge Roy Johnson. He was now Warden W. W. Waid's headache.

Frazier decided to test his skills in escaping the Texas Prison System in the Walls Unit. Frazier had numerous escape attempts and pitched gun battles under his belt, and he seemed to have no fear of being shot or shooting in return. To Frazier, gunplay was part of the job in escaping. His body was said to hold more lead than any man alive. Whether that was true or not, Charlie had born many bullet wounds over the years. Somehow Charlie Frazier had so far evaded a death sentence for himself. During all of his exploits, Frazier never was sentenced to the "hot seat," the outlaw lingo for the Texas electric chair.

Before the Death House Escape, Frazier had already tested the waters at the Walls Unit. Frazier started the new year with a bang on January 13, 1934, in Huntsville, Texas. With two other men, he attempted to escape using a ladder against one of the walls. A guard saw the group and fired, hitting Frazier in the shoulder. Frazier and his partners were put in solitary confinement. All this was going on at about the same time Clyde Barrow, Floyd Hamilton, and James Mullins were working out how to raid the Eastham Prison to rescue Ray Hamilton and Joe Palmer.[8]

It is clear that Frazier still had escape plans despite his earlier failures, as well as Lee Simmons' personal warning to him regarding his conduct. Frazier and four other inmates, including Roy Thornton, Bonnie Parker's husband, tried to escape again using a ladder against a wall. Two picket guards caught the men in a crossfire, killing one, seriously wounding another, and almost killing Frazier with a wound just over his heart. Although not expected to survive, Frazier spent weeks in the prison hospital, where he met Whitey Walker.[9] Incidentally, Bonnie Parker never divorced Roy Thornton. She thought that divorcing Thornton while he was still in prison would not be morally right. Even when she was killed with Clyde Barrow, she wore her wedding band.

That completes the cast for the Texas Death House Escape on July 22, 1934, the most dynamic and crow-eating escape in the history of the Texas penal system.

One must first understand the mentality and the amount of desperation for those individuals involved in the Death House incident. The convicts in the Death House Escape were a "who's who" of outlaws. While in the hospital at the Walls Unit, Walker told Frazier he wanted to save his friend Blackie Thompson from the electric chair.[10] Frazier was more than willing to offer his services to implement a plan.

To understand how the July 22, 1934, escape could have happened, one should be introduced to prison guard Jim "Boss" Patterson. Patterson was a charismatic forty-two-year-old who was good at his job when he was sober. Patterson was intelligent, and to ease the boredom of his guard duties he conversed with members of the prison population. Before his prison job, Patterson had worked as a foreman in Mount Vernon, Texas, as superintendent of maintenance in eight counties with headquarters in Paris, Texas, ending in 1925. He was foreman from 1926 to 1932, when he was fired for drunkenness. He was out of work for a short time until he was hired as a guard in the Texas Prison System in December 1933.[11]

For the first three months after he went to work as a guard in the Texas Prison System, he worked the picket on the south wall, and then for a while carried a squadron to the construction of the stadium near the walls. For three months, ending in July 1934, he was in charge of the sawmill located in the lower yard of the industrial section. In all fairness to Patterson, most of his version of the events that prelude the escape parallels other sources that testified regarding the breakout—that is, with the exception of how the pistols were smuggled onto the prison grounds.

This is how Patterson described his involvement in the matter as he was interviewed doing his own prison time in 1934 after his conviction as an accomplice in the escape:

> There seemed to be plenty of money floating around in the Walls. Many of the inmates seemed to always have plenty of money, and a pool of betting was being operated by various inmates involving baseball games. On two occasions I bet $20 and lost both times.
>
> On one occasion while in the Walls hospital, Whitey Walker, who was in the hospital at the time, asked if I would mind doing him a favor. Walker said that he wanted $1,000. With this he was going to break the pool that had been betting on baseball games. In order to do this, I would carry out of the Walls a letter written by Walker addressed to a man named Thompson at Weatherford, Texas. I mailed this letter at the Huntsville post office. I read the letter and it stated that Walker needed $1,000, and the letter instructed Thompson to meet me and give me the $1,000.
>
> About two nights later, at a given signal, two honks from a horn, I met Thompson, and received $1,000 in currency done-up in a package. I examined this package and saw that only money was in the package. I brought this package into the Walls and delivered it to Whitey Walker in the Walls hospital.
>
> I met Thompson and received the package at the forks of Highway 75 and the west part of Huntsville, where the Dallas Highway and the Navasota Highway forks off. After delivering the entire $1,000 to Whitey Walker, I reported back to my job at the saw mill and one Lloyd Johnson, a ball partner of Walker, delivered $500 in cash to me. All these transactions took place in the week prior to the break from the death cell, which happened on one Sunday, late in July 1934.
>
> I decided that I needed to go on a party with a friend of mine in Paris, Texas. I went to Paris and had a wild drinking party with my friends and returned to Huntsville the following Friday after the break had been made.

It was determined later that an escaped hard case named Austin Avers, with the aid of Estelle and Dorothy Davis (the Davis sisters), made the gun arrangements with Patterson.[12] It is widely speculated that the Davis sisters also drove the two get-away cars. Through the prison grapevine, Walker got word from Palmer and Hamilton to count them in.[13]

Hugh Kennedy had jumped from one fire to another. He had been moved from Eastham to the Walls for protection in exchange for testifying against Hamilton in shooting guard Bozeman at the Eastham Raid in January. In the courtyard of the Huntsville prison stood a gazebo. As some convicts loitered around the gazebo, talk of a breakout was murmured through the ranks. Kennedy told one of the men, "You guys can't make it. I came here during the day. It's farther down on the backside than you think. Plus, there's a little ditch on that far end."[14]

There was a baseball game being played during the Walls Death House prison break at the stadium next door. The prison team, the Tigers, were playing the Humble Oilers baseball team.

Lee Simmons had talked to the print shop superintendent a few days before the Sunday of the baseball game. Mr. Barnett, the superintendent, was concerned about events going on at his shop. Some inmates were trying to tunnel out of the print shop. They had dug down through the concrete, dug a well, and were tunneling out.[15] Simmons and some prison help caught the prisoners in the process of tunneling. They were naked, maybe to avoid getting dirt on their white clothes, and the tunnelers were ordered to lockup by Simmons. When Simmons, Albert Moore, and Barnett left the print shop, they passed Charlie Frazier on the side of the archway walking west toward the toilets. Unknown to the prison officials at the time, Charlie already had three pistols concealed on him as the prison officials headed to the ball game.[16]

According to Lee Simmons, although Frazier handled the gun details, the break was planned by Walker.[17] As Simmons was busting tunnel escapes and Charlie was moving guns, Whitey Walker had been sitting around all morning on the east porch. Still nursing a broken arm from the shotgun blast, he was allowed to recuperate at the hospital by sitting in the sunshine and fresh air.[18] The plan had already been set in motion. As Roy Johnson told the story to Warden Waid later, Whitey was to be out on the hospital porch and some cars were to come. After the necessary arrangements were made, the people in the car would

drive around and blow their horn. In return Walker was supposed to wave at them. (The prison hospital is a multi-story
building that would enable him to be high enough to be seen
over the wall). After this was done, the cars drove to the back of
the dog kennels and waited until it was time to move. The Death
House occupants knew what was going to happen that morning
because inmates on the outside could talk to them in "Dog
Latin," a practice that was common but not understood by just
anybody.[19] The Whitey Walker Gang used this technique in the
Caldwell Jewelry kidnapping.

There once had been a guard twenty-four hours a day at the
Death House, but the convicts would act up more when a guard
was present than not, so that practice had been stopped.[20] While
Simmons and most of the Walls prison population were at the
baseball game near the prison, guard Lee Brazil started toward
the Death House door. The guard had brought the evening
meals, which were carried by two trustees, as he unlocked the
door to take the food inside the corridor. As he turned around
to lock the door on the outside, a stripe-clothed Charlie Frazier
put a gun on him and said, "Don't holler or press the button or
I will kill you."[21]

"Give me the keys," Charlie barked, and then made one of
the stewards unlock Blackie Thompson's cell. The gunman
placed the guard in Blackie's cell, and then he released Palmer,
then Hamilton. Frazier wasn't happy about releasing Hamilton,
but Palmer reminded him about the youth's role in the Eastham
Raid. Charlie then sent the trustees into Raymond's cell.

"Anyone else?" Frazier asked. The other two condemned
men, Pete McKenzie and another man named Rector, declined.[22] McKenzie had been on death row for twelve years, and
his real name was John Daniel McKenzie; he was an icon in the
system. According to an article written by Harry McCormick,
who was one of the most prominent prison reform journalists of
the 1930s, McKenzie was both a cop killer and escape artist. His
role in the 1934 Death House Escape has always been over-
shadowed by the involvement of Walker, Patterson, and Frazier.
McCormick states that McKenzie was five-foot-seven and
weighed 130 pounds. His small stature allowed him to crawl
through a barred window after he was smuggled a key for the

padlock on his cell from the steward's office. Keys were then made in the machine shop, the impressions made of the locks on the doors for the men who intended to escape, thereby explaining how the condemned men opened the locked cells during the escape. ("Death of Texas Convict Opens Secret of Escape," written by McCormick as a news staff writer on June 26, 1965) Although this contradicts other testimony, it should be remembered that Lee Simmons refused for McKenzie to give testimony to the Prison Board after the break, thinking he wasn't trustworthy enough.[23]

Frazier, Hamilton, Palmer, and Thompson ran from the Death House and were joined by Whitey Walker, Roy Johnson, and Hub Stanley.[24] The seven men moved to the picket at the entrance to the lower yard, where they rushed guard W. G. McConnell, forcing him to come along at gunpoint.[25] What had become a small mob picked up two other convicts in the lower yard and locked them up in the dark room of a Captain Baughan's office.[26] They broke the lower yard gate lock and ran to the machine shop. In the machine shop, Walker grabbed some bolt cutters and then led the men to the fire house, using the cutters to break a chain that secured an extension ladder. They were about thirty steps from where they came around the building to the Walls.[27]

Hugh Kennedy didn't go to the ball game that day, and he watched the men running through the courtyard in the direction of the back wall. *It's higher than they think,* Kennedy thought as the inmates ran. There probably weren't over a dozen people inside the Walls during the baseball game.[28] They made their way to guard Carey Burdeaux's picket station number seven in the southwest corner of the lower wall.[29]

Guard Burdeaux was sitting in his picket and heard convicts talking within the walls. When he went outside of the picket on the platform, someone said, "Hands up."[30]

"Death cell prisoners first," Frazier told the group.[31] Hamilton was the first up the ladder, taking Burdeaux's pistol as he passed by. Then came Palmer, who took Burdeaux's rifle, then Blackie Thompson. The picket guard was told to lie down, and by this time the escape was noticed by another picket. As Hamilton, Thompson, and Palmer were going down the outside stairs, they heard three shots. Hamilton and Palmer continued down, but Thompson went back to the picket to return fire. Guard George was grazed in the head by a bullet that probably came from Blackie's rifle.

At the same time another guard, W. W. Roberts, was also about 150 yards from Burdeaux's picket, and he could see that five convicts were now armed and some were returning fire.[32] Guard Roberts immediately called the front and told them there was trouble at number seven. The next man up the ladder was Frazier, but picket eight guard Ed Roberts saw what was happening and starting shooting from 150 yards away.[33] Roberts then shot Frazier, who was dressed in prison stripes, and the man fell to the ground. After Charlie Frazier was shot, Whitey went for it. He did what he could in climbing the ladder but was hindered by his broken arm. It has been said that Roy King, a convict working in the hospital, had taped a pistol to Walker's hand so he could fire without dropping the weapon.[34]

Walker, halfway up the ladder, said, "God, it looks like we're gone." At that moment, guard W. W. Roberts shot Walker, the bullet entering his right side and coming out the left, penetrating the convict's lungs.[35]

As Whitey Walker fell, he reportedly shot into the ground.[36] The body was released to Forgner and Gresham Undertakers, in Huntsville, Texas, with a single gunshot wound.[37]

Thompson started shooting at guard George, not knowing that his friend Whitey was dead, trying to keep the guards off of him to get back to the ladder. George had shot his rifle three times from the number six picket, but when the bullet grazed the side of his head he got down, and by that time the shooting was over.[38]

Frazier started up the ladder again, and Roberts pumped another bullet into him. He fell to the ground, shook off the effects of the round, and went up a third time. Roberts shot him again. This time Charlie swung around under the ladder, and the guard shot him a fourth time.[39] Blackie Thompson ran back down the steps toward the waiting getaway cars.

The last one to try to escape on the ladder was Roy Johnson, and after he received a flesh wound for his efforts he surrendered. When Roberts had emptied his gun, he called the front again. In all, Roberts shot nine times; he attempted to reload his rifle, but he could only get one cartridge in it. When his rifle was empty, he picked up a shotgun and fired it until it snapped.[40]

Hub Stanley discovered real quick that he didn't want any part of what was going on, so he ran behind some cordwood and a house where a pump was located and joined guard McConnell, who also chose that spot for cover.[41] For some reason, perhaps sheer vengeance, Blackie Thompson again returned to the picket and started shooting at Roberts, who had made his way toward Burdeaux's picket along the wall. When he missed with his last rifle round he pulled a .45 automatic and emptied it at Roberts. His final act of defiance was to throw the pistol at the guard and run down the stairs for good to a waiting vehicle.[42]

The three men who had successfully made it over the wall jumped on the running board of a car and the car sped to freedom.[43] Roberts was still on the wall and grazed Hamilton in the foot before the car was gone.[44] One of the cars took the turn at Fourteenth and Avenue J on two wheels, so fast that it almost turned over. The two cars headed north on Highway 75.

In the meantime, in the bottom of the ninth inning at the ball game with two strikes on the batter, Lee Simmons and Warden Waid heard the start of a pitched gun battle at the far end of the prison. Simmons and Waid ran from the ballpark to Burdeaux's picket, climbed the stairs, and saw Walker dead in the courtyard and Frazier on the stretcher, being taken to the hospital. By the time they got to the prison yard, Waid told Simmons to look, and when he looked down the side of the building he could see the death cell door standing open.[45] For the second time in seven months, Palmer and Hamilton had escaped from a maximum security Texas prison.[46]

Realizing what had happened, Simmons went to make some dire phone calls, asking the telephone operator to stay on the line. She first connected him to Dallas, then Corsicana, Bryan, and also Lufkin. She then received instructions for call connections in San Antonio, Shreveport, and Houston.[47] Simmons didn't know how the pistols got to the escaped prisoners but was fortunate when a friend phoned him about one of his guards throwing money around in Paris, Texas.[48] Because of the call, Simmons sent for Jim Patterson. After a few questions from Simmons, Patterson got evasive. Simmons questioned him about how he had been free with his money in Paris.[49] Patterson claimed that he had borrowed $500 from his uncle John, paid the bank $100, and paid a $50 grocery bill. Simmons dismissed Jim from the room, pretending to believe him. Simmons immediately called his friend in Paris and asked him to call Patterson's Uncle John and inquire about the money. Within thirty minutes Simmons got a call back.

"Lee, that's a fine old man. He told me that he had heard his nephew was here, but that he didn't see him or let him have any money." Simmons sent Albert Moore to check up on Jim, and Moore returned with a full report, including a list of Jim's expenditures.[50] Simmons summoned Patterson back, but he was missing. Patterson had gone to Madisonville, thirty miles north, to call a lawyer and have him visit Patterson's Uncle John and convince him to confirm Jim's "loan" story.

Jim returned at 6:00 that evening, but Simmons and his secretary, W. C. Watson, were waiting for him. By that time, Simmons also had a note that Jim had written to Roy Johnson, saying, "I'm hot. They think I had something to do with it. Tell the officials the guns came through the ballpark. Tell them there is another gun hidden in the ballpark. Tell them anything to take the heat off me, and I may be able to help later on."

Even after a severe verbal drubbing and confrontation over his story versus the note by Simmons, Patterson kept to his story. Simmons and Luther Berwick took Patterson to Grimes County and put him in jail, incommunicado, under the care of Sheriff Harrington.[51] After a night and a day in jail, Patterson weakened, first admitting to smuggling letters into and out of the prison for $500, then finally, the following day, acknowledging his complicity in the whole affair.

On the Friday night before the break, Patterson had received three guns from someone he claimed he didn't know. On Saturday he brought the guns into the prison through the east gate while riding on a wood wagon. He hid the guns in his office, from which he supervised the wood yard and sawmill, where Frazier later picked them up.[52]

Upon telling his side of the story later, Patterson related a different version of events. His statement was written by a prison official:

> The subject states that he was first questioned by Warden Waid and was arrested on these charges on about August 3, 1934, at his home in Huntsville. He was taken to Houston, retained overnight in the death cell, and brought back to Huntsville Unit under heavy guard for further questioning, after which he was taken to Anderson, Texas, in Grimes County.
>
> After he was seen there by various prison officials, he finally dictated a statement, which he signed, giving information essentially as described above.
>
> However, he stated that Warden Waid had changed the statement to say that he brought in guns in the package containing the money, rather than money itself. He absolutely denies this is true. At the time of his trial he was advised to plead guilty to three charges of aiding prisoners to escape: Whitey Walker, Charlie Frazier, and Raymond Hamilton. He states that he realizes that this was a mistake. He claims that at the time of the trial the judge said something about the fact that the sentences were listed in the court records as not running cumulative. However, the commitment papers read that the sentences were cumulative, totaling 15 years.

The prison official added their own conclusion to the interview:

> Although the information was not verified, it was rumored that two Davis sisters, who had been connected with the men who escaped, were keeping company with the subject at the time he passed the letter out, brought the money back in, and that they had probably been drinking with him, living with him, and probably sleeping with him. The Davis girls were supposed to be the ones who furnished the money and the guns. This rumor was not known to the interviewer at the time the subject was interviewed. Even though the subject was requested to give full details concerning the offense, he mentioned nothing about the Davis sisters.
>
> Jim Patterson, after pleading guilty to the charge of aiding the escape of prisoners, received three five-year sentences in Walker County.[53]

In a final note on McKenzie, he was eventually paroled in 1957, but according to McCormick's article, he had become so institutionalized that he requested to be taken back to prison. The prison board refused and sent him west for a better climate for his asthma, where in Olympia, Washington, he took part in an armed barroom battle. His parole was revoked, and he died of emphysema at the prison hospital sometime between 1960 and 1965—records are sketchy.

Charlie Frazier was a special guest in the Death House, probably in the special meshed cell four. As for the three men from the Death House who made it over the wall, Hell was coming to breakfast in Texas.

CHAPTER 14

The Aftermath

After the carnage of the Death House Escape, Blackie Thompson, Ray Hamilton, and Joe Palmer were on the loose. Whitey Walker was dead, with a bullet through both lungs. Charlie Frazier had been shot four times and eventually joined Hub Stanley in solitary confinement. Roy Johnson had been slightly wounded and served many years before being sent back to Oklahoma to finish his original sentence there. In 1945 he was paroled and disappeared from public view. A cousin of Roy's was some sort of movie producer, and Roy's prison files are sprinkled with letters to the warden from him on Roy's behalf. The youngest of the Fishing Hole Gang calmed down after his partners were gone, and short of some laziness problems, lived out the rest of his prison time uneventfully.

In Rogers, Texas, Whitey's body laid in state at a relative's home. It was estimated by the July 25, 1934, edition of the *Houston Post* that about five hundred people came to pass the casket of the dead outlaw. Whitey Walker's niece, Ruby Lauderdale, said in a 1976 interview that the three escapees from the Death House took their chances with so many police looking for them in Rogers to pay their respects to their fallen friend before the fugitives went their separate ways. According to Ruby, Blackie Thompson had been shot in the leg, and while

151

a doctor treated the leg Hamilton and Palmer ate fried chicken that a local church had cooked for the grieving family.[1]

After they went their own ways, Palmer was the first to be recaptured. On August 8, three weeks after the break, he was in Paducah, Kentucky, again, just like he was after the Eastham Raid when Bonnie and Clyde rescued him. He had collapsed from sheer exhaustion, the result of not sleeping for days. He went to sleep near some railroad tracks with a loaded .45 by his side. A passerby thought Joe was a corpse and called police. Two officers came up and kicked his pistol away. "The Lord had his arm around those two cops," Joe was quoted as saying. "If I hadn't been dead tired for sleep, you'd have to bury them."[2]

At first, Paducah authorities thought they had nabbed Alvin Creepy Karpis, a leader of the Barker Gang. Proper identification was further complicated by the fact that Palmer had mutilated his fingerprints by rubbing them on concrete until they were virtually unrecognizable.[3]

"You've got my picture," said Joe. "Now find out who I am on your own."

The following morning, an anonymous caller suggested that Chief of Police Bryant read a certain detective magazine to figure out the identity of this mystery man. A full-page story about the escape from the Texas Death House told Bryant everything he needed to know. Within a week, Joe Palmer was back in Huntsville.[4] Bud Russell spent most of his life transporting prisoners to Walls in Huntsville. In his unpublished autobiography, "Uncle" Bud recounts his thoughts on Joe Palmer as he escorted the Southwest's number three badman back to the Death House:

> Again I was detailed to return Joe to the Death House at Huntsville. By agreement with Colonel Simmons, my son, Roy Russell, now Assistant Night Warden at Huntsville, was to accompany me. After accomplishing what was apparently an impossible feat in the Death House Escape, the prison officials felt justified in doubling all precautions to ensure Joe's positive return; and I could not have asked for a more dependable and trustworthy officer to side me, should anything go amiss, than my son, Roy.
>
> Conveying those who have been convicted to prison and escorting recaptured convicts from points all over the nation, Canada, and Old Mexico back to prison have long been duties

of my day's work. But, even so, on very few trips have I failed to become interested in one or more of my passengers, sometimes for personal reasons; but more often regarding their religious prospects and spiritual welfare. Returning an escapee from the very jaws of the Electric Chair was far from being an ordinary occurrence in my regular routine of duty, but as we boarded the train in Paducah for the return trip to Texas, I found myself again probing my mind for words that could find their way to the heart of this boy, whose latest episode had emblazoned his name across the headlines of newspapers from coast to coast, labeling him one of the deadliest menaces known to present-day society.[5]

Raymond Hamilton went back to his old game of bank robbing. After he had taken several hundred dollars from a Continental oil station near Dallas and robbed the First National Bank of Carthage of $1,000, a trap was laid for him. In a South Dallas apartment, city police and federal officers waited for Ray and Floyd, but something went wrong when the brothers arrived at 10:30 one night and escaped despite heavy gunfire.[6] Two weeks later, Raymond and an accomplice (probably Hilton Bybee) broke into the National Guard Armory at Beaumont and stole eight automatic rifles. The next week, Constable John Record and some highway patrolmen engaged Hamilton in a gun battle at McKinney, from which he escaped again. Fleeing from McKinney, he and his partner abandoned their car, kidnapped a farm boy, took his car, and then entered the farmhouse of Will Mays, near Celina, Texas, where they stood guard over the family throughout the night. The next morning the outlaws stole another car and took the three hostages to Fort Worth, finally releasing them in Cowtown.[7]

On March 28, 1935, Hamilton and Ralph Fults robbed a bank in Prentiss, Mississippi, locking five people in the vault and taking $1,100. They had a female getaway driver, and when they changed cars outside of town the Davis sisters had their hands in the action again. They were waiting for Ray and Ralph with a fresh car. The women went their own way and were captured by Sheriff Mathison of Jefferson County, Mississippi. Hamilton and Fults were forced to shoot their way out of several entanglements, which led to the kidnapping of some law enforcement members to act as human shields. By the time the two men had reached Memphis, Tennessee, the National Guard and hundreds of local officers were guarding all highways in the vicinity. Fults ended up back in Texas alive, but not before he had also been hit with a shotgun blast in his back.[8] Hamilton had left Fults in Memphis, and from there the Southwest's most wanted man headed for the train tracks to hop a freight train. Soon he encountered a group of hobos, including a teenage runaway named Noland. Hamilton was still wearing a three-piece suit and a fine Stetson hat, when he talked to the runaway.

"Say, buddy," Ray smiled, eyeing the kid's knapsack. "You got another pair of them overalls?"

"Sure do," Noland answered.

"I'll give you ten bucks for them," Ray said.

"Okay," said the youngster.

"You want to ride with me?" the outlaw asked, watching a line of boxcars rolling past.

"Sure," said Noland. "I ain't got nothing else to going."

Hamilton and Noland picked out a car and hopped aboard, sliding onto the rods so the freight detectives wouldn't spot them.[9] On Thursday morning, April 4, they arrived in Fort Worth's East Belknap switching yard. Raymond sent the runaway into West Dallas on Friday morning with the hopes of arranging a meeting with his mother, something Fults had warned him against doing. Knowing that Noland could neither read nor write, Ray wrote a message on the back of a discarded envelope and handed it to the runaway. The teenager had difficulty locating the address furnished by Hamilton. Unsure of his destination, he asked a cab driver to cruise through the neighborhood that was in the general vicinity of where Ray had told him to go.

Timing was not good for the boy, because three county detectives named Bill Decker, Bryan Peck, and Ed Castor watched the taxi driving aimlessly through West Dallas. After watching the car for several minutes as it turned in and out of side streets and narrow alleys, the deputies decided to find out what this was all about.

"What are you doing, son?" asked Decker.

"A friend of mine over in Fort Worth asked me to deliver this note," said Noland, offering the folded piece of paper to the deputies. After reading the message, they took Noland in for questioning. The lawmen produced a mug shot of Raymond Hamilton and stuck it in the boy's face.

"That's the guy that's waiting for me. What did he do?" Noland asked innocently.

"Do you mean to say you don't know who this is?" asked one of the officers skeptically.

"No," said Noland. "I ain't got no idea."[10]

"Will you show us where this man is waiting?" another deputy asked.

"Yes, sir," Noland agreed reluctantly, "I guess so."

At twilight a group of lawmen assembled in front of the Rock Island terminal. Noland led "Smoot" Schmid, Bill Decker, and a five-man squad of officers to the edge of the railroad yard. About fifty yards away the group could see a tin shed where Hamilton and a half dozen hobos stood. Raymond's back was turned toward the officers. He was dressed in a pair of greasy overalls, a brown vest, and a brown hat.

"Go on over to him," Decker told Noland. The Mississippi runaway slid down the embankment and walked toward Ray. Before Raymond could turn around and say anything to Noland, seven automatic pistols were pointed at his back.

"Hoist 'em, Ray," said Bill Decker, a .45 pistol accenting his meaning to the outlaw. Hamilton complied without a show of resistance. A strange smile flickered across his lips.[11]

So at 7:00 P.M. Friday, April 5, 1935, Raymond Hamilton was captured at Fort Worth after a nine-month search across the country. Also taken into custody was a twenty-nine-year-old man of Springfield, Illinois, named Glen Allen. He was held for questioning. Hamilton was armed with two .45 caliber pistols and three extra clips, all loaded. He only had a few dollars, but he hadn't lost his flair for dressing well. The contents of his black suitcase were a new suit, shoes, pajamas, safety razor, and soap.[12]

Three and a half months after Palmer was arrested, Amarillo police got word that Blackie Thompson was using a house in town as his base of operations. The house was kept under surveillance while waiting for Thompson. A black Ford V-8 rolled up in front of the house on the evening of December 6, 1934, but the driver quickly sped away.[13]

When officers first learned that Thompson was in the area, extra guards staffed the banks as an added precaution. It had been rumored for days that the outlaw was intending to rob a bank in Amarillo.[14] Later in the day on December 6, Thompson was driving along Amarillo's East 10th Street in a car he had stolen from E. L. Turner of McLean, Texas. At 6:40 P.M., Amarillo police chief W. R. McDowell recognized the fugitive as he and Detective Clark Cain were cruising the vicinity.[15] The chase was soon taken up after the police chief's finding had been conveyed by radio to other police scout cars and to the sheriff's department.[16]

Police scout car number four, driven by Sid Harper, pulled up beside Thompson's car and ordered him to stop. Blackie replied with a wild pistol shot toward the officer. The bandit floored the gas pedal and headed for the highway.[17] Outdistancing the officers, he turned onto North East Eighth Avenue and sped eastward on Highway 66, continuing east with speeds up to eighty-five miles per hour.[18] Crude radio equipment called in other lawmen as things got desperate for Thompson. Soon there were ten lawmen chasing Blackie. As the armada of cars neared the Amarillo city limits, Potter County Sheriff Bill Adams came in behind Thompson's, but he was still far behind the outlaw in the chase.[19]

Deputy Sheriff Roy Brewer opened fire on Thompson's car with a rifle, and one of the bullets crashed through the rear glass of the sedan and went out through the windshield. Still far away from Blackie's car, Brewer squeezed off another round and struck a rear tire, making Thompson's car careen off the highway and skid along the barrow pit for possibly fifty yards. This created a cloud of dirt that veiled Thompson vehicle from officers' view.[20] As soon as the sheriff could stop his car, he turned toward where the outlaw's car had gone off the road and focused the lights on Thompson. The escaped convict never missed a beat. He quickly got out of his car, carrying a shotgun, rifle, six-shooter and a bag of ammunition. The lights of Blackie's car were turned off.[21]

Sheriff Adams got out of one side of his car and Deputies Brewer and Ivy Wilkinson exited the other. They opened fire almost at the same time that Thompson leveled a shotgun at them. Thompson's shot went wild—he was blinded by lights of the sheriff's car—but one of the officers' bullets struck him in the leg. The Death House escapee managed to get two shotgun blasts off, one missing officers by inches and spraying glass everywhere.[22] He had also emptied the contents of a .45 pistol besides the sawed-off shotgun during the three-minute standoff. He was reaching for his .30-30 rifle when deputy sheriff Gib Landis opened fire with a machine gun, hitting Blackie in the chest and face. Deputy Sheriff Brewer managed to get within a few feet of Thompson and pumped bullets into the outlaw with his .45 revolver.[23] He died instantly.[24]

It was rumored that an informant had told police contacts where the outlaw would be that evening in Amarillo. Despite overcomming numerous life and death situations before, Blackie Thompson slumped face first in the dirt near the disabled car, his body riddled with seventeen bullets.[25] He was killed at 7:05 P.M. that Thursday night but had managed to give ten city and county officers a fifteen-mile chase all the way from downtown Amarillo to a field off Highway 66. The body was sent to Shamrock on a Rock Island train by N. S. Griggs & Sons, and then taken overland to Wheeler.[26] That was not the end of the story, however.

Unlike many other outlaws of the period, Thompson did not take his associates anywhere near his parents' home, thereby making it hard for police to track him. The police were used to looking for the Whitey Walker Gang, not a lone figure traveling to visit his family. Blackie wouldn't talk about his legal problems; in fact, he spoke little to anyone.[27] Like many other desperate people on the run, family was important to him, and protecting family was equally important. Bringing a harboring charge on loved ones was a risk that was just taken to secure the family bond. So one can imagine what Blackie's brother and nephew must have felt when that train pulled up to the station in Shamrock. It was not the fact that the body was brought by train, it was specifically how it was done. His clothes had been stripped off his body, a flat board put on a freight car, and his bullet-ridden corpse was sent packing. That is how his family found Blackie when his remains were sent to them.[28]

When they got his body home, he was cleaned up and

dressed as best as the family could do. The body of the outlaw was laid in a coffin in the children's bedroom overnight until the funeral. There was one blemish, a bullet hole they couldn't seem to cover in his forehead.

"If I knew who put that bullet hole in his head I'd kill the son of a bitch!" his father, W. J., wailed in grief.[29]

A nephew of Blackie's, W. J. Ford (named after his grandfather), remembered that night sixty-five years ago. "Uncle Irvin and I had played many a game of dominoes," Ford recalled as he looked over a freshly cut coastal grass field from his porch. "We never called him Blackie unless he made us mad. You should have seen my grandfather's face that night. He and I stayed up all night by the coffin talking. It really took a toll on him, the way that whole thing was done. They were good people, and I hate to see any of them hurt."[30]

As the *Amarillo Daily News* wrote in the December 8, 1934, edition, "Justice of the Peace C. W. Carder, holding his first inquest, returned a verdict stating that Thompson died of 'bullets fired by officers in the line of duty' while he was resisting arrest. Soon after the inquest, the body was taken to the Griggs chapel. Yesterday, the public was barred from viewing the body, upon orders of the family."

Raymond Hamilton and Joe Palmer were sent back to the Death House, their escape cutting off any hope of appeal. Short of the parole board or the governor, it was over for these two badmen. Palmer appeared to resign himself to the inevitable, but Hamilton became nervous and restless as the execution date grew nearer. Palmer tried to quiet him, telling him that he might just as well take the situation as it was and prepare for the ordeal that was to follow.[31]

Hamilton had completely lost any facade of nerve when his final day was almost at hand, and he now looked for comfort from the same man he had once tried to kill. Palmer's calmness gave Ray a sense of dignity in accepting the fact he was about to die. Although Joe had once said he couldn't stand to be near Ray any longer, he now took on the role of his spiritual advisor.

Even the choice of who would go to the chair first Palmer left to Raymond, but Warden Waid thought it best to send Joe first, and that is what happened.[32] Newspapermen wanted an interview with Palmer, but he told them he wouldn't believe a newspaperman on oath and that he didn't want them to know anything about his life or family. He went on to explain that he had intended to be killed rather than captured and electrocuted, for his little sister would have a hard enough time without having it advertised that her brother had been put to death in the electric chair. He reluctantly gave reporters an interview after they gave their word that his family would not be included at all.[33]

Public sentiment was leaning toward having Ray's sentence commuted to life imprisonment. By April 17, in Houston alone there were ten thousand signatures on a petition calling for Governor Allred to commute the sentence, but the governor chose not to intervene. It was lights out for Hamilton.[34] While Raymond was lodged in the Death House cell at Huntsville, a Dallas psychiatrist warned that "all children are potential Raymond Hamiltons." For professional reasons, the psychiatrist asked that his name not be revealed. His warning was specific:

> This man who now faces death is distinguishable from a huge mass of delinquents only by the degree to which he has gone and the publicity which he has received. In his effort to overcome a feeling of inferiority, probably generated by his physical smallness, he had overcompensated; he has tried to make himself the most feared man in the Southwest. That is illustrated by two things. The first is that he has steadfastly maintained a spirit of braggadocio. The second is that he has continuously, in the face of tremendous odds, and showing lack of judgement, come back to the vicinity of Dallas where he could strut in front of those who knew of his supposed prowess, and who gave him a type of hero worship.[35]

Charlie Frazier was not forgotten during all of this, certainly not by Lee Simmons. After being thrown into a death row cell, Simmons made it clear that if Charlie wanted to try and escape again, there would be no mistake as to who he was; Frazier was not allowed to shave. He was weak, unkempt, and grossly underweight. Harry McCormick interviewed the escape artist shortly after the resignation of Lee Simmons. Neither his hair nor his beard had been cut in months, and he appeared unwashed as well. McCormick wrote that Frazier "looked and walked like a fugitive from the grave." Not long after the interview, Frazier was transferred back to Louisiana, where he received a life sentence for his part in the prison break at Angola in 1933. In perfect Charlie Frazier fashion, he tried to escape again on October 18, 1936. The man was shot six times at close range and still he lived. He spent the rest of his life preaching after a conversion to Christianity.[36]

Joe Palmer was reviewing his life as well as thinking about the afterlife. In a never-before-revealed letter from Joe Palmer, "Uncle Bud" Russell shared Palmer's request for his presence at his execution as well as his thanks:

> Captain Bud and Roy Russell.
> Dear Sirs:
> As you probably know I will soon start that short walk which ends at the electric chair. Before that time comes, I am very desirous of thanking both of you for the kindness and consideration shown me since my arrest in St. Joseph, Missouri, for the murder of Major Crowson.
> I would like you to know that I expected you to accord me the treatment you did, for I don't think it possible for a man to reject a lifelong principle in one moment.
> At the same time, I well realized that if you had chosen to murder me, you could have done so without suffering any ill consequence for the act; and in all probability you would have received the plaudits of the thoughtless populace.
> I also know, if you had been desirous of acquiring a killer reputation, you would not have waited thirty years to take up that ignoble pursuit of notches.
> I think there will always be a demand for the policeman who is willing to commit murder; but I think the day is not far advanced that all intelligent men will recognize the fact that laws must be elastic enough to even include law enforcement agencies. Blood has begot blood from the earliest date in world history; it will continue to do so, unless [the] law of average crumbles, which is to say, if God takes his hand from the helm. When I was arrested in Kentucky I intended to protest extradition, and when I finally consented to return to Texas without extradition, it was not because of any desire to save the state of Texas the expense of obtaining extradition through legal channels.[37]

I think I can truthfully say, if anyone other than you two men had come after me, I would not have waived extradition. I also want to thank you for the courtesy you extended my little sister at my trial in Anderson.

There are, I suppose, people who would have looked on her with malice; however, I think your consideration of her at all times proves that you did not. I would like for you to know she was not there because she approved of outlawry, but because she was willing to face the eyes of the morbid curious rather than see me face death alone. I am afraid this is a very poor effort in return for all kindness and consideration you have shown me, but I am grateful even if I cannot express myself clearly. I would appreciate it very much if you can be here at my death, for if you are, I believe I can say I have two more friends in the death chamber.

Most Respectfully,
Signed—[Joe Palmer][38]

Right before midnight, the main gates of the Huntsville prison swung open and the masses waiting to see Palmer and Hamilton die in the electric chair started coming through in an orderly fashion. Then the ghoulish desire to be close to the action took over, the same way people slow down to see the blood and gore in a horrible automobile wreck. The crowd raced one other to get close enough to see, but to their dismay the spectator section was already packed with state legislators and other special guests with advance ringside seats.[39]

People rushed for the open door, crashing though at a rate of two and three bodies at a time, grumbling and shoving as they fought each other for a place to stand, stoop, or kneel. It was time for Joe to go through the green door. Now that he was done picking through his final meal of fried fish, ice cream, and chocolate cake, he gave Hamilton a last goodbye. Prison officials along with Father Finnegan approached Joe, who had converted to Catholicism.

He walked through the green door, and that was the end of Joe Palmer. Pat Byrd, whose father was an executioner many times in later years, said the worst part wasn't the convulsions of the man in the chair, but the stench that stayed in the area for hours.[40]

A few minutes later, the handful of prison officials and designated guards arrived before cell number seven. Raymond Hamilton, the top of his head shaved smooth, looked up.

"Is Joe . . . gone?" he asked.

Father Finnegan nodded. Moments after Joe's body was taken away to the mortuary, Raymond was taken to the death chamber. He went out in style, wearing his own monogrammed blue silk shirt and autumn brown jacket. One leg of his matching trousers had been opened at the seam so that the proper attachments could be placed on the condemned man's shaved left ankle.[41]

His head was then drawn tight against the chair and tied in place by a strap. Star-shaped copper electrodes were strapped to Hamilton's skull and left ankle. So that his head wouldn't fuse to the metal cap, a piece of brine-soaked organic sponge separated the metal from his bare skin. Then a chin strap was tightened on the young man's face.

"Well, goodbye all," he said as the leather mask covered his face.[42] It would have taken fifteen seconds for the heavy jolt to take effect. The rest of the process goes like this: The body tightens, and the wrists spring the hands straight up in the air as far as the leather bands allow for movement. The back starts to arch, and soon the strapped-down convict will involuntarily relieve his bowels. In the second stage, the voltage is dropped way down because the skin is starting to smoke. So for another fifteen seconds this is a slowing down of the process. The third fifteen seconds calls for a spike in the voltage, but not enough for the eyes to jerk from their sockets. In the fourth and final stage, the juice goes up again, but not enough for the condemned to catch fire. Sometimes, they are still alive when the minute is up, and the heart beats for a little while.[43]

Sunday Morning with the Warden

Warden Jim Willett leaned over the front of his desk in the Walls Prison Unit and shook my hand. "Do you want some coffee before we go over there?" he asked me. I told him that I was fine, that I had made the trip from Texas A&M to Huntsville in just under an hour, drinking coffee all the way. The "over there" the warden referred to was the execution chamber. People have different names for it: the gurney room, the lethal injection area, the final death row, and so on. I just call it the execution chamber. This was not my first trip to the chamber with the warden, but today was completely different. This was not a brief glimpse at the area for me, not on this visit. It was Sunday morning, and the warden had agreed to explain start to finish what had to be done on execution watch, the day a death sentence was to be carried out on a condemned prisoner for his crimes.[1]

Jim usually smiled and joked with me when I came to ask his advice on the Walls penitentiary. He was a veteran of the system and had worked his way up through the ranks over many years in a variety of duties. Many of the mysterious questions regarding the prison's past kept Jim Willett looking for answers, those same answers that helped me find the truth regarding the men behind the 1934 Death House Escape. It was not very far from his office that the event occurred. This morning the warden did not smile. He took his coffee cup, thought about a refill, and declined. "Let's go," he said. It was time for the warden to explain to me what arguably the hardest job in the world was like, at least for a few days a year. Like two days earlier, when a young man was strapped to the gurney to pay for a crime so heinous it is not fit to describe here. We left the administrative area, and I signed the in/out sheet on a desk near a set of bars that open the "Bullpen." Upon entering the Bullpen, we took a side trip through the original Wall wing that at one time housed Union prisoners of war. Three stories high, the walls are so thick that it is cool inside while the sun burns brightly outside, even in the summer. At the end of this now-abandoned structure is the solitary metal box that once held the notorious badman John Wesley Hardin. On the other side of the wing, Chief Santanta was held on the third level, kept in prison as a criminal instead of a prisoner of war. The chief took a swan dive from the top of an adjacent building—whether with or without help is debatable. We crossed the courtyard, the climax location of the 1974 Carrasco siege that ended in tragedy. Across the yard, one can still make out the bullet holes in the wall. I could see the infirmary steps where Whitey Walker and Roy Johnson passed the time waiting for Charlie Frazier to make his move on Guard Brazil.

By this time, a guard was summoned to unlock a couple of gates, and once they were opened we walked down a sidewalk past some rosebushes. The warden told the guard he could leave, and we looked at the steel door that kept us from the inside of the building we had come to see. Warden Willett unlocked the door and pulled it toward us. There is a certain smell to the area when a person walks in and looks at the facility. I remember that Jim once told me that he could be blindfolded, walked all over the prison, and he could stop and tell you when he was in this building. It does not have any special disinfectants, but everything about the chamber is absolutely sterile. Nothing is out of place. There is not any dirt. The paint is fresh and a light color. When first entering the building, one is at the near right end of the wing. A closed metal door is to the immediate right, and eight cells in a row are to the left in a corridor layout. The first cell (all cells are unnumbered here) has a fine metal mesh that ensures the condemned has no way of receiving anything through the bars. This is the visitor cell. To the left and across the corridor of what I will call cell two is a half table and two chairs. Next to that table is another table with a vase and artificial flowers. I think this disturbs me more than anything in the entire setup. I feel like I am in a mortuary. The strange and unexplainable doctor's office smell, artificial flowers, clean, sterile, white tablecloths, and farther down the row there is a pulpit. At the end of the row next to what I call cell eight is yet another table, with a telephone sitting on top of it. One of the cells has no bunk in it. During death watch, only one prisoner is allowed in this area at a time, so I couldn't understand why there are so many cells. The warden cleared his throat. I turned on my recorder and asked the first question:

PATRICK McCONAL: *Tell me about death watch—let's start from the time you wake up in the morning. You've got to get up, you know you've got a long day, it's six in the morning or whatever—what happens from the time you shower? You know this is going to happen, this is going to happen tonight.*
WARDEN JIM WILLET: To be real honest with you, I dress a little nicer those days. I don't know if it isn't as much for the inmate as it is for—you know, I think we all look our best with all the media and the public around. But I come up and generally have a normal day up until 9:00 A.M. A little after 9:00 I call Austin to the Attorney General's office and ask them if there's anything pending on this case. They'll tell me. If it's in the courts, you may be looking at a long day.

Are people trying to constantly get through to you during the day?
Trying to find out about it? Well, what I do, Pat, when I get off the phone with the Attorney General's office, I've got a list of all those people, from Wayne Scott down to if you want to call it the littlest person, which is probably the most important person. I call all of those people as soon as I get off the phone with the Attorney General's office. It usually takes me thirty minutes to an hour, depending on how much conversation we have.

I notify all these people, 'Hey, I just got off the phone with the Attorney General's office, and this is what's happening.'

Now on days that I may call all those people and tell them, hey, they're in the Fifth Circuit and you know when they get through there, we're going to wind up in the Supreme Court with them. If I have one of those days, yeah, I have people that are just curious that I work with that's calling all day wanting to know, 'What's the latest you heard?'

Have you actually had one go down to the eleventh hour?
     Well, we think of that. I don't think with our modern communication that's very likely that's ever going to happen. If we show up at—if they tell me we are in the courts at 9:00 A.M., I call back at 2:00 or 3:00 P.M.—Yeah, we're in the fifth circuit now, we just got out of there, and we're fixing to go to the Supreme Court with it.
     At about 5:45 P.M., I'll call back for sure, if I even wait that long and find out, but at 5:45 for sure, I'll call back and they say, 'Hey, the Supreme Court's had it for an hour, it's probably going to be awhile.' We don't do anything, we sit up there and wait for a phone call from the Attorney General's office to either go do it, or don't. There's no use to come back here and upset the inmate and sit around back here with nothing more to do than you can do up front.

Where are the witnesses at this point?
     They're across the street. We basically don't have 6:00 P.M. at that point until they call and say it's okay or its not okay. So if they call, and it may be 7:30, and they say, 'Hey, he got a stay,' well, then we call Ellis Unit I and say you need to come pick the guy up.

What happens from that end? When does the condemned arrive?
     They usually bring him in the early afternoon. They'll come in our back gate and get him in here. They'll get him in here and get him out of his clothes and get him clothes that we've got for him—just as a security thing. Make sure he hasn't got anything hidden. He'll bring his property with him if he's got it. We'll set it over to the side and they take him down and thumbprint him for ID Purposes. Then we put him in the next to the last cell down there at the other end. That gives the chap-

lain a little bit more privacy with him throughout the afternoon. We always had them up at the first cell until a few months ago. Everybody coming and going right by there while he's trying to have a serious conversation with the guy wasn't working, so we changed it and it's worked out real good.

After they get him in the cell, they'll call me and sometime in the next few minutes, I'll come back here and we talk. I don't mind telling you from my point of view, it's mainly just to try and feel this guy out and see how he's going to be. I've had some good conversations with these guys, some humorous conversations, some of them have a good sense of humor and a good personality.

I'll go over things with them, like what are you going to do with your property, who's going to claim your body, what happens with your money? Just general conversation about stuff like that. Are you expecting any visitors this afternoon? Do you want a phone call? I'm pretty free with the phone calls. If they want to call somebody, a cousin or somebody they haven't talked to in years, or somebody that didn't want to come to be a witness, or if they didn't want to invite him, I'll let him have some phone calls.

They can have a spiritual advisor visit for thirty minutes here in the afternoon. We'll bring them up and put them in the visiting cell with the screen. They can have their attorney for thirty minutes sometime during the afternoon if they want to. Generally that doesn't happen. More so the spiritual advisor than attorney. The attorney is probably busy someplace else and we let him have the phone call. If the attorney calls and wants to talk to him, we put it through. I've been pretty liberal with phone calls. I don't see that it hurts anything. It probably settles them some.

What about the last meal?

Prior to him coming over here, I'm talking about a week ahead of time or something in that nature, Ellis prison will ask him what he wants for his last meal. He'll tell them to make whatever and they relay over here what he wants to eat, so we know days before he gets here what he wants to eat. He eats here in the cell. This thing gets a little bit rearranged sometimes, but they'll usually move a table down here and you'll have tea and coffee and water, and they've got all sorts of snacks for him and the employees who are going to be back here all afternoon.

They usually eat about 4:00 P.M. and I will tell you that it is amazing to me sometimes how much, I mean, these guys will order two cheeseburgers and french fries and I'll get back here and maybe while they are on the gurney, I'll ask the chaplain, 'What about his meal?' 'He ate every bit of it.' You'd be surprised how many of those guys can eat a humongous helping two hours before they know they are going to die. I've always felt like if I knew that, if it was me, somebody brought food in front of me, I'd probably throw up.

Is it really a choice of what you want for a last meal?

We try to do that. Apparently, when they had the electro-cutions, they pretty much tried to give them what they wanted. We are limited these days, and a guy may ask for a steak, but we don't have any solid meat anymore, it's all ground up. So, if they ask for a steak, we try to fix 'em up a good smothered steak or hamburger steak.

What about drinks? Tea or whatever?

We'll get them Cokes or something if they want that. We try to accommodate those things that we can.

No alcohol, right?

No, although some request a beer.

Is it difficult to supervise this process?

It's not that I'm supervising these people. The hardest part for me is the fact that some of these guys have great personali-ties. They've obviously changed, appear to be very changed. I mean I don't know what they were like back then, I've read about it, and they appear to have gotten it all together and are fun to be around. I don't know any other way to say it. The chap-lain has told me some of his best afternoons have been spent with these guys. The hardest part is you come in here and see a guy like that and hell, he's healthier than you and I are, and you know in another twenty minutes he's going to be dead as this floor. It's just a sad thing.

Well, can you walk me through the process?

He comes in, they are going to have him all shackled up. Feet, hands, everything. They'll take him out of his shackles and clothes. They'll give him his underwear, and he'll go over there and do his fingerprints. When he gets through there, they'll put him in this cell and hand him his clothes and he'll get dressed.

Usually, within five to thirty minutes I'm going to be back here and talk to him. We talk about what I've told you before. One of the things, when we get through with that part, I'll usually tell him you know, I'll say, "Look now," and I'm honest, "is there something going on in the court, do you think this is going to happen? Do you think this is going to go off tonight?" And I'll always tell them, "Regardless whether in court or not, and nothing happens to change this thing, to change this thing between now and six o'clock, at about six o'clock I'm going to come through that door and tell you come on out of the cell and go in the next room. It's up to you, you can go on your own or we'll help you." 99.9% of them will tell you, 'Oh, you don't have to worry about me, I'll go back there on my own.' That's always good to hear.

I can't think of some of the things I've joked with them about. When I come back to talk to them, there's usually my assistant warden, the major, plus the three supervisors that are already back here. The warden and the two assistant wardens from Ellis and maybe their major will be here and come back here with me, so I've got a crowd—not that I like to get in front of a bunch of people, but they get amused at me sometimes at some of the things that I talk to the inmates about.

I got back here one day, and had a guy back here, and I did all the talking. I got ready to go and I started to walk off, and I remembered there's a strange thing about this one. Today was his birthday. I turned around and said, "Happy Birthday." And he said, "Well, thank you." And they all got a kick out of that. I was sincere, I wasn't funning the guy. In fact, we got that guy a cake and brought it back here. They baked a cake for him and brought it back here and found a candle for him to blow out.

We try and be accommodating. I have had some of them back here, on the gurney, after they've been strapped down and it's just me and him and the chaplain, while we're waiting on the witnesses to come. I've had several of them tell me that they really appreciated the staff here being kind to them here the last few hours. So we have a good staff that are not abusive towards them.

Who can the condemned visit with before the execution?
The preacher or lawyer, that's all he's going to see. The family's out once he gets here. Everybody is out, nobody else is going to talk to him—if they do, it's going to be on the phone.

Have you ever had a situation that two are due for the same day?
We bring them over one at a time. When we get through with the whole thing, at that point when the funeral home is going to pick up the body, we'll call Ellis and tell them to bring the next guy. Now the next guy in that situation, and it's just how it happens, he gets a little screwed in the deal. He doesn't have a nice quiet afternoon with the chaplain and all that stuff. He doesn't, but that's just how it's set up to be.

Anyway, they're going to get the inmate out and ask him if he wants to shower. If he showers, he'll come and go in this cell right here. He'll wait with the chaplain here then. The chaplain will be right out here all the time. So around 4:30 he gets to take a shower, and then they'll move him in here.

We got one over here one time way back and somebody called me. I'm thinking this guy had a hold on his account, or showed that he was in debt to the state, which generally means that he has broken some property, torn up some property, and we charged him with it. This happens with these cases so when money comes in, instead of him getting it, it goes towards paying for whatever. Well, this guy had gone on a rampage several years before this and tore up a TV. He was in debt for the TV, and I asked somebody, "How come he owes money?"

"Oh, he tore up a TV, but he's changed now, he hasn't given us any problems in three years."

I told him, "I want you to know now that I found out about you." We had this radio here, and I said, "Usually, we have the radio there, and there's a TV up there for you to watch, but I found out about you and you are not tearing my TV up." He went to laughing, and everybody in here got a big kick out of it

—just something to try and loosen the guy up a little bit. He went along with it. He thought that it was funny I knew about him tearing up that TV.

He's eaten and now he's in cell two, what we'll call cell two. It's 6:00 P.M. and it's time. You know that because you're in your office and you start your walk over here through that catwalk back there. That takes you into that little room. This guy knows that it's about 6:00 and everybody knows it's time to take care of business. What happens when you walk out of that room?

I'm sure the chaplain has told him when he's asked, if he's asked, what time it is. Remember that I told you that people split up? Well now, there's going to be the guy that works that door, plus the wardens from Ellis Unit and people like that; there's a few of those people when I go back this way, and I'm sure he can hear me and my people walking behind his cell. There's all these people, and they are suddenly going to come in. He's got to know at that point that it's getting pretty close.

At about five minutes until six, I'm usually sitting in my office. I'll get up and get my jacket on and everybody follows me, that's just kind of what happens. When we get back to the area just behind that wall, there'll be people that'll break off and come to this cell block like you and I did. I and some of my bosses, and I'm talking about my bosses, the people up above me, will come back through here and be in that medical room there. When we get in here, there's a phone in there. The ringers turned off of it, and there's a light on it. We watch for that light, and when it lights up one of my supervisors will answer the phone. The first call is always from the Attorney General's office, and they typically will say that it's okay to go forth with the execution, that there's nothing pending. They will hang up, and the people in the warden's office and assistant warden's office will put through a phone call immediately from the governor's office, and they get the same word from them usually. When that happens, I come back and go into the cell block. We'll go into that first cell past the visiting cell, we've moved him down there by then. I'll tell him that it's time. Generally the guy's sitting down, he'll get up and walk to the cell door and he follows me in here, and all of them are right here with him when he comes.

We get in the gurney room and I usually stand right here. The inmate will get up, and we tell them that they have to get on the gurney and lay down; one of the officers will tell him. We have nothing but supervisors, sergeants and above, working back here. He'll lay down and they'll have the straps undone. They'll go to strapping him in a matter of a few seconds, thirty seconds probably. They've got him strapped in and I'll check the straps and get a feel for them and they're always right. I'll ask the inmate when I get up here closer to his head, "Is this uncomfortable for you? Are any of these straps uncomfortable for you?" We'll make adjustment's if they are; I never have had one tell me that they're uncomfortable.

At this point I'll tell the officers thank you and they'll go on back into the cell block area. That door at that time is usually just barely open at that point. The medical people know that they can come out. I'll open the door and they'll come out here and start putting IVs in him. Generally what I do when that's going on, if they start over here, I get over there and I try to get the inmate's attention on me and we talk. Most of them go along with that. I think they're happy to have somebody to talk to them at that particular point. A few of these guys come in here scared to death of needles. I have really tried to carry on a good conversation just to get their mind away from that needle fixing to go in. And so when they get the one in over here, then we'll swap places, I'll come over here and get the guy attention this way and talk to him about whatever. I've talked to him about God, I've talked to them about their children, I've talked to them about their drug problems on the streets, whatever they want to talk about at that point. I've had a couple or three don't want to talk about anything. I don't force them into it.

They will insert a needle here and they start with just a saline solution flowing. They will go over and hook another one up for backup purposes if something goes wrong with the first one. There are two lines that run through there, one to this one and one in under here, through here and it'll hookup to a needle here. Once the guys get that done they go back into the medical room and close the door behind them.

I'm usually here still talking to the inmate and the chaplain will be here. When that happens, we have a fellow who usually sits right by the door, and he's got a speaker and we've got the microphone out and the speakers on. One of the last things that happens while they're in here putting the stuff in the needles is, one of the people that works here will come in and pull a microphone down and get the sound system going. The speakers in each one of these rooms are for the witnesses. The guard sitting at the door, he'll come on and tell them that it's time to bring in the witnesses.

They bring the victim's witnesses first and put them in that room. When they get them in here and the door is secured, then another bunch, some of my people, will bring the inmate's witnesses, and put them in this room here. They never cross paths.

At the same time I'm also going to have some internal affairs people, a Texas Ranger, a major and a captain, and five people from the media in here with these people. Sometimes they may all be over here if the inmate doesn't have any witnesses and I'll put all the media over here.

There's not a limit on your number?

Yes, the inmate can have five plus a spiritual advisor, and the victim's witnesses can have five. There's five media and then of course our security. Sometimes there are our media people and our victim's services people, so sometimes it can get crowded. They were talking about remodeling this thing, and my point with it is that you probably use it ten hours a year. You figure from the time we get those phone calls in here at 6:00, most of the time by 6:20–6:25 at the latest, it's over with. So you're talking about from 6:00, we get the phone calls, we get the guy from the cell, strap him down, put needles in his arm, and then call for them—how long are they in there? Maybe ten minutes. They can be uncomfortable for ten minutes as far as I'm concerned, it wouldn't bother me if I were one of them.

So we get those witnesses in and generally when they come in, the chaplain is back at the foot and I will usually get out of their way. When they get in, one of my bosses will open that door. It's a ritual thing. I told him here a while back I could do this thing without him; they'll open the door once everything is secured, and one of them tell me, "Warden, you may proceed."

Same thing 200 times, same words every time. Maybe a different person, but the same words.

At that point I usually tell the inmate that it's time that he
can make a statement if he'd like. Generally from that afternoon,
or sometimes in here, he's told me what his last lines are going
to be. So he will make a little statement. I have seen some of them
who wouldn't say anything, just shake their head, or they don't
want to say anything. Just one or two, three, something like that.
It has also been to the point that I've seen them say their sorry to
each one of these victim's witnesses in here and then turn and
talk to each one of their witnesses separately in there.

I have told them early in the afternoon that you can make
a statement, but let's hold it to three or four minutes. I have had
two that I had to wrap it for them. One of them was to the point
here a while back that I had to clear my throat a couple of times,
then I finally just stepped over and when he took a breath, I told
him that's enough—he was going on for a long time. Anyway,
when we get to that point, where he lets me know that he's
through, I give a signal to the people in the one-way glass.

Who all is behind the one-way glass?

My immediate boss, and at least one of his bosses. That person is the one who usually steps out and tells me to proceed. You
have a person who is the key man that lets us back through and
takes care of locking the doors. You will generally have two medical people back here. That's generally who's in there, about
four or five people. I've also seen that room very crowded when
board members may show up and I don't have room for them,
so we have to put them in the witness area.

So what happens when you do give the signal?

When I give them the signal they start the stuff flowing.
We've got a couple of guys that will come out here and get the
needles hooked up, and then there is one person, if you want to
say the executioner, the one who actually pushes the drugs
through, there's one person that does that.

How does that work?

They have the stuff hooked up back there. They are flowing

a saline solution and when I give the signal, then they put this first stuff through. They tell me we give them enough to put a horse to sleep. Then they put this saline solution back through, a little bit of it in there to flush the lines, and then they put the other solution in that stops the lungs, and then they put the one in that stops the heart. I can tell you from watching this that generally from the time I give them the signal until that guy takes his breath, he'll usually take a kind of a labored last deep breath, and at that point it usually takes about twenty-five seconds.

You can still see after that some pumping of blood, but when they give me the signal and let me know that they got all the stuff in the body, I was told and always do, count off three minutes from that time. I can tell you the first time I did that, that was the longest three minutes that I thought could possibly ever be. It seemed like an hour.

Is the chaplain still in here?

Yes, he and I and the inmate. By the time they give me the signal, it's all over in principal purposes. That guy is gone.

How do you get the signal? Do they open the door?

No, that little window, and this has been this way for years, they've got a roll of tape in there, just regular medical white tape, and they'll open that door and stick that tape in there and then close that door. I don't know if anybody's ever noticed. I notice it so much because I watch for it. I count off three minutes from then. When that three minutes is over, I turn around and open the door. The doctor is standing out there. He is not one of our employees, he's on contract and he will come in here while me and the chaplain are still here. He will take a flashlight out and look at the eyes. Then he will feel for any pumping at the neck, then he'll take the stethoscope and put it on and check his heart. When he does that he'll tell me it's 6:22, for example. Then he turns around and leaves. I usually move the microphone out of the way, and I'll repeat that message so that the news media, if they didn't catch it, can hear me say into the microphone, it's 6:22.

At that point, they open that door and start taking the people out. They get one room out and then they get the other

room out. Once they are out of there, I go and open the door.
The medical people come in and take all the needles and stuff
out. Then the officers come back in and they unstrap him.

On execution days we have a big tarp we put up on that
fence outside so people can't see through. Just on the other side
of that, there's a hearse. By now, we've already told the people
from the funeral home the situation and they are waiting right
outside the door. They'll come in here with their gurney and put
the body on it and away they go.

Sometimes, I guess, you've had a few that have made a scene?
We had some people show up, a dad and some brothers,
and obviously they'd had a few drinks, and they got a little abusive with their language back here. An inmate's brothers and
dad. Now, we tell them up front that if you come here and we
smell alcohol on you, or you're not acting sober, you're not
going in. Some others have fainted, and some have cried out.

The chaplain, when does he leave?
He's here with me until the very end. He is probably the key
to this whole thing. If he's able to get to the inmate and have a
good afternoon with him, it helps, you can tell. I think most of
the guys that come in here, they've been knowing for a long time
that they are going to die today and they've gotten themselves
right with the Lord, and they are pretty much at peace with
everything. The chaplain does a great job of keeping them that
way or getting them even more so.

How many of these do you think you've had to do?
I don't know. I really don't. I know we've done about nine
this year and we did about twenty last year. I had three before
that. I guess I'd have to say about thirty-five. They are a hard
thing to watch.

*Have you had people call you wanting to watch an execution who are
not directly involved? In other words, wanting to watch for kicks, or just
to say they saw one?*
Anybody who has called me about wanting to view the
thing, I've referred them to my superiors. I've told them that if

you're not one of the witnesses picked then you are not going to be there. I'm really not the one to make that decision. If they are adamant about wanting to talk to somebody, I've referred them to the proper channels. We, the people that work back here with me, other than those two people who were contracted, all the rest of these people are volunteer people. Quite a few people, after the Carla Faye Tucker execution, decided they didn't want to do it anymore. I'm talking about some people who never had a problem with any of it before.

Does it feel to you like it's a ritual now?

No, they are all different. I guess the fact that you're dealing with a human being here that is fixing to be put to death … I did it one time, early on, I got the records out and read all about this horrible crime this guy did, and then I got back here and he didn't seem to have a very good personality. I didn't have a good conversation with that guy and I thought I'm not going to do that again. I've got a job to do and it needs to be done as best I can do it and I can't read about how these guys committed these horrible crimes and then come in here and do my job the way I want to do it.

*   *   *

I left the Walls Unit that morning near noon and thought about what I had heard the warden tell me. He would finish his shift and probably go home. I would drive the hour back to my house and think about the gurney, Whitey Walker, Joe Palmer, Hugh Kennedy telling me one of the most dramatic stories I was ever privileged to hear, and remember the stench of the chamber. I would think of a walk through vines and thistles with a woman in her eighth decade kind enough to show me a kidnapping site. Old banks, the Texas Panhandle, the pine forests of East Texas, the ruins of Old Eastham would dance in and out of my memory. Old files with the smell of molded edges, Internet searches, backwoods interviews, lost transcripts in watermarked boxes in warehouses, all of these things I have encountered to bring this story to print. I don't know if I left a rekindling of times for these people or the opening of old family wounds that had finally been healed or at least forgotten. Maybe I did both, but the story is told and I am now putting it to bed.

In the words of the outlaw journalist Hunter S. Thompson, "It never got weird enough for me." For this writer, *this* story was pretty damned close . . .

Endnotes

CHAPTER 1:   WHITEY WALKER AND THE EARLY YEARS
   1. Jerry Sinise, *Black Gold and Red Lights,* 47.
   2. Eloise Lane, "The Day They Robbed the Bank in Pampa," 4.
   3. Sinise, *Black Gold and Red Lights,* 57.
   4. Lane, "The Day They Robbed the Bank in Pampa," 4.
   5. Sinise, *Black Gold and Red Lights,* 57.
   6. Ibid.
   7. Ibid., 58.
   8. Ibid., 58.
   9. Ibid., 82.
  10. Ibid., 60-61.
  11. Lane, "The Day They Robbed the Bank in Pampa," 7.
  12. Sinise, *Black Gold and Red Lights,* 63.
  13. Ibid.
  14. Ibid., 82.
  15. Ibid., 82.
  16. Lane, "The Day They Robbed the Bank in Pampa," 20.
  17. Sinise, Black Gold and Red Lights, 82-83.
  18. Texas prison records of Whitey Walker.
  19. Sinise, *Black Gold and Red Lights,* 83.
  20. Ibid., 84.
  21. Ibid.
  22. Ibid., 85.
  23. Ibid., 85.
  24. Oklahoma prison records of Whitey Walker.
  25. Sinise, *Black Gold and Red Lights,* 86.
  26. Lane, "The Day They Robbed the Bank in Pampa," 42.
  27. Ibid., 45.
  28. Ibid., 45.

CHAPTER 2:   THE REST OF THE CREW
   1. Texas prison records of Roy Johnson.
   2. Texas prison records of Roy Johnson.

3. Texas prison records, Roy's side of the story as told to prison officials.

4. Oklahoma prison records of Roy Johnson.

5. Texas prison records of Roy Johnson.

6. Texas prison records of Roy Johnson.

7. W. J. Ford, interview by Patrick M. McConal. July 8, 1999. Schulenburg, Texas. Ford is Blackie Thompson's nephew.

8. Texas prison records of Irvin Thompson.

9. James M. Day, *Captain Clint Peoples, Texas Ranger: Fifty Years a Lawman*, 39.

10. Ibid., 38.

11. W. J. Ford interview with author.

12. Ibid.

13. Ibid.

14. Oklahoma prison records of Irvin Thompson.

15. W. J. Ford interview with author.

16. Texas prison records of Irvin Thompson.

17. W. J. Ford interview with author.

18. Day, *Captain Clint Peoples, Texas Ranger: Fifty Years a Lawman*, 37.

19. Ibid.

CHAPTER 3: ROGERS BOUND BUT BUCKHOLTS WILL DO

1. Day, *Captain Clint Peoples, Texas Ranger: Fifty Years a Lawman*, 37.

2. Ibid.

3. Ibid., 37-38.

4. *Temple Daily Telegram*, October 7, 1933.

5. Ibid.

6. Ibid.

7. Ibid., October 8, 1933.

8. Ibid.

CHAPTER 4:   HIT AT PALESTINE

1. Sue Bonner Thornton, *The Bonner Family History*, 148.

2. *Palestine Herald*, October 27, 1933.

3. Thornton, *The Bonner Family History*, 149.

4. This doesn't match other statements of what happened, but it is possible that Enoch was referring to himself since he was the first person in the bank. That would explain why other bank employees were able to move after the thieves left the building.

5. *Palestine Herald*, October 27, 1933.

6. It is unclear what area was actually robbed since the words "vault" and "safe" are used synonymously.

7. *Palestine Herald*, October 27, 1933.

8. Ibid.

9. Ibid.

10. Thornton, *The Bonner Family History*, 149.

CHAPTER 5: THE CALDWELL JEWELRY STORE ROBBERY

1. Mable Doerge, interview by Patrick M. McConal, October 8, 1998.

2. *The Bryan Daily Eagle,* December 15, 1933.
3. George Hamilton, "Lawman and Outlaws," 284.
4. *The Bryan Daily Eagle,* December 1933.
5. Ibid.
6. Hamilton, "Lawman and Outlaws," 285.
7. *The Bryan Daily Eagle,* December 15, 1933.
8. Hamilton, "Lawman and Outlaws," 285.
9. *The Bryan Daily Eagle,* December 15, 1933.
10. Ibid.
11. Ibid., December 16, 1933.
12. Hamilton, "Lawman and Outlaws," 285.
13. Ibid., 286.
14. Judge Tom McDonald, Jr., interview with author, March 12, 1999.
15. McDonald interview.
16. Sam Fling, interview with author, October 6, 1998. Fling was the jeweler for the Caldwells from 1943 to 1987. John Sealy Caldwell related the robbery event to him.

CHAPTER 6: ON TO MARLIN
1. *The State of Texas v Irvin (Blackie) Thompson,* Statement of Facts by M. V. Bradshaw, 11.
2. *The State of Texas v Irvin (Blackie) Thompson,* Bradshaw, 12.
3. Ibid., 13.
4. Ibid., 33.
5. Ibid., 32.
6. Ibid., *14.*
7. Ibid., Statement of Facts by Miss Andrew Peyton, 3.
8. Ibid., Peyton, 4.
9. Ibid., 5.
10. Ibid., Bradshaw, 15.
11. Ibid., Bradshaw, 16.
12. Ibid., Peyton, 6.
13. Ibid., Bradshaw, 17.
14. Ibid., Bradshaw, 17.
15. Ibid., Peyton, 6.
16. Ibid., Peyton, 7.
17. Ibid., Bradshaw, 17.
18. Ibid., Bradshaw, 18.
19. Ibid., Peyton, 7.
20. Ibid., 8.
21. Ibid., Bradshaw, 19.
22. Ibid., Bradshaw, 19.
23. Ibid., Bradshaw, 20.
24. Ibid., Bradshaw, 21.
25. Ibid., Bradshaw, 21A.
26. Ibid., Peyton, 9.

CHAPTER 7: JOE PALMER AND RAY HAMILTON MAKE THEIR DEBUT
1. Martha Palmer, interview with author. Palmer is Joe Palmer's niece. August 8, 1999. Hillsboro, Texas.
2. Prison records of Joe Palmer.
3. S. E. Barner,"Hell-Bent Joe Palmer," 58.
4. Barner,"Hell-Bent Joe Palmer," 58.
5. District Court of Limestone County, Texas records.
6. Texas prison records of Joe Palmer.
7. Barner, "Hell-Bent Joe Palmer," 58.
8. Ibid., 59.
9. Ibid., 59.
10. Ibid., 60.
11. Ibid., 60.
12. Sid Underwood, *Depression Desperado*.
13. Ibid., 1.
14. Ibid., 2.
15. Ibid., 4.
16. Ibid., 4.
17. Ibid., 4.
18. John Neal Phillips, *Running with Bonnie and Clyde*, 66.
19. Texas prison records of Raymond Hamilton.
20. Phillips, *Running with Bonnie and Clyde*, 100.
21. Ibid., 100.
22. Ibid., 100.
23. Texas prison records of Raymond Hamilton.
24. Phillips, *Running with Bonnie and Clyde*, 119.
25. Ibid., 119.
26. Ibid., 124.
27. Underwood, *Depression Desperado*, 38.

CHAPTER 8: RABBIT RUNS AT EASTHAM
1. Hugh Kennedy, interview with author, July 30, 1999.
2. Ibid.
3. Ibid.

CHAPTER 9: WELCOME TO THE 'HAM: PRELUDE TO A RAID
1. Mullins' prison interview statement, Texas prison records.
2. Texas prison records of James Mullins.
3. *The State of Texas vs. Hilton Bybee*, testimony of Ernest Slape, 3.
4. Ibid., testimony of Maud Hood, 14.
5. Ibid., Hood, 14.
6. Ibid., testimony of Anna Renfro, 9.
7. Ibid., Renfro, 9.
8. Ibid., Slape, 4.
9. Ibid., Slape, 5.
10. Ibid., Slape, 5.
11. Ibid., Slape, 5-6.
12. Ibid., Slape, 6.

13. Ibid., Slape, 4.
14. Ibid., Renfro, 10.
15. Ibid., Renfro, 9.
16. Texas prison records, French's statement of events to prison officials.
17. Texas prison records of J. B. French.
18. Ibid.
19. Ibid.
20. Ibid.
21. Ibid.

CHAPTER 10: "HE DIDN'T GIVE ME A DOG'S CHANCE"
1. Kennedy interview, July 30, 1999.
2. Ibid.
3. Ibid.
4. Texas state climatology facility, Texas A&M University.
5. *The State of Texas v. Joe Palmer,* Mullins transcript, 8.
6. Ibid., Mullins transcript, 9.
7. Ibid., Mullins transcript, 9.
8. Ibid., Mullins transcript, 10.
9. Ibid., B. B. Monzingo transcript, 22.
10. *The State of Texas v. Joe Palmer,* 10.
11. Ibid., Mullins transcript, 10.
12. *The State of Texas v. Joe Palmer,* 10.
13. Ibid., Monzingo transcript, 21.
14. Kennedy interview, July 30, 1999.
15. Ibid.
16. Ibid.
17. *The State of Texas v. Joe Palmer,* Bozeman transcript, 23.
18. Ibid., 26.
19. Ibid., 24.
20. Kennedy interview, 30 July 1999.
21. *The State of Texas v. Joe Palmer.*
22. Ibid., Bozeman transcript, 25.
23. Ibid., Bobbie Bullard transcript, 27.
24. Ibid., Bullard transcript, 27.
25. Refugio County records, no. #831, Henry Methvin, judge's instructions to the jury, 1.
26. *The State of Texas v. Joe Palmer,* Mullins transcript, 11.
27. Ibid.
28. Kennedy interview, 30 July 1999.
29. *The State of Texas v. Joe Palmer,* Bozeman transcript.
30. Lee Simmons, *Assignment Huntsville: Memoirs of a Texas Prison Official,* 116.
31. *The State of Texas v. Joe Palmer,* Brew Hubbard transcript, 18.
32. Ibid., Mullins transcript, 12.
33. Ibid., Hubbard transcript, 19.
34. Ibid., Mullins transcript, 12.
35. Kennedy interview, July 30, 1999.

36. Ibid.
37. *The State of Texas v. Joe Palmer,* Mullins transcript.
38. Ibid., Monzingo transcript, 22.
39. Ibid., Bozeman transcript, 24.
40. Ibid., Gordon Burns transcript, 30.
41. Ibid., Burns transcript, 31. This is Crowson's dying statement.
42. Ibid., Burns transcript, 31.
43. Ibid., Mrs. Walter Crowson transcript, 32. Mrs. Walter Crowson was his mother.
44. Ibid., Veazey transcript, 33.
45. Ibid., Veazey transcript, 36.
46. Ibid., Dr. Anderson transcript, 37.
47. Ibid., Anderson transcript, 38.
48. Kennedy interview, 30 July 1999.
49. Simmons, *Assignment Huntsville: Memoirs of a Texas Prison Official,* 116.
50. Ibid., 118.

CHAPTER 11: THE GETAWAY
1. *The State of Texas v. Joe Palmer,* Mullins transcript, 12.
2. Ibid., Mullins transcript, 13.
3. Ibid., 171.
4. Underwood, *Depression Desperado,* 43.
5. *The State of Texas v. Joe Palmer,* 172.
6. Ibid., 172.
7. Underwood, *Depression Desperado,* 46.
8. *The State of Texas v. Joe Palmer,* 172.
9. Ibid., 172-173.
10. Ibid., 174.
11. Underwood, *Depression Desperado,* 48.
12. Ibid., 49.
13. *The State of Texas v. Joe Palmer,* 178.
14. Ibid., 180.
15. Ibid., 181.
16. Ibid., 181.
17. Ibid., 182.
18. Ibid., 182.
19. Ibid., 183.
20. Underwood, *Depression Desperado,* 55.
21. Ibid.
22. Ibid., 56.
23. *The State of Texas v. Joe Palmer,* 190.
24. Ibid., 191.
25. Ibid., 192.
26. Ibid., 194.
27. Ibid., 188.
28. Ibid., 195.
29. Simmons, *Assignment Huntsville,* 166.
30. *The State of Texas v. Joe Palmer,* 197.

31. Ibid., 198.
32. Phillips, *Running with Bonnie and Clyde*, 206.
33. *The State of Texas v. Joe Palmer*, 199.
34. Simmons, *Assignment Huntsville*, 134.
35. Ibid., 142.
36. Phillips, *Running with Bonnie and Clyde*, 311.
37. Ibid., 311.
38. Ibid., 311.
39. Texas prison records, J. B. French.
40. Texas prison records, J. B. French.
41. Texas prison records, Hilton Bybee.
42. James Mullins interview with prison officials June 3, 1938.
43. Mullins interview with prison officials, Texas prison records.
44. Texas prison records, James Mullins.
45. Phillips, *Running with Bonnie and Clyde*, 222.
46. Ibid., 223.
47. Ibid., 224.
48. Ibid., 224.
49. Ibid., 224.
50. Ibid., 224.
51. Ibid., 224.
52. Ibid., 224.
53. Simmons, *Assignment Huntsville*, 141.
54. Ibid.
55. Underwood, *Depression Desperado*, 123.
56. Bud Russell, unfinished manuscript, 8.
57. Phillips, *Running with Bonnie and Clyde*, 224.
58. Ibid., 225.
59. Max Rogers, interview with author, Huntsville, Texas. November 4, 1998.

CHAPTER 12: BUSTED IN FLORIDA: THE BEGINNING OF THE END
1. *Marlin Daily Democrat*, January 25, 1934.
2. *The Bryan Daily Eagle*, December 30, 1933.
3. *Marlin Daily Democrat*, January 25, 1934.
4. Ibid., January 26, 1934.
5. Ibid., January 29, 1934.
6. Ibid., January 29, 1934.
7. Ibid.
8. Ibid., February 7, 1934.
9. Ibid., January 29, 1934.
10. Ibid., February 7, 1934.
11. Ibid., January 30, 1934.
12. *The Bryan Daily Eagle*, March 15, 1934.
13. *Marlin Daily Democrat*, January 31, 1923.
14. Ibid., February 5, 1934.
15. Ibid., February 13, 1934.
16. Ibid., February 13, 1934.

17. Ibid., March 2, 1934.
18. Ibid., March 7, 1934.
19. *The Bryan Daily Eagle,* March 6, 1934.
20. Ibid., March 7, 1934.
21. *Marlin Daily Democrat,* March 9, 1934.
22. *The Bryan Daily Eagle,* March 8, 1934.
23. Ibid., March 9, 1934.
24. Ibid., March 12, 1934.
25. *Marlin Daily Democrat,* March 12, 1934.
26. Ibid., March 13, 1934.
27. *The Bryan Daily Eagle,* March 15, 1934.
28. *Marlin Daily Democrat,* May 9, 1934.
29. Ibid., March 17, 1934.
30. Ibid., March 30, 1934.
31. *The State of Texas v. Irvin (Blackie) Thompson,* Statement of Facts by
F. H. Lambert, 42-46.
32. *Marlin Daily Democrat,* March 31, 1934.
33. Ibid., March 2, 1934.
34. Ibid., June 4, 1934.

CHAPTER 13: OVER THE WALL
1. Pat Byrd, interview with the author. Huntsville, Texas. 1999.
2. Joe Bauske, interview with author, May 22, 1999.
3. Peter D. Tattersall, *Conviction.*
4. Simmons, *Assignment Huntsville: Memoirs of a Texas Prison Official,* 171.
5. Ibid., 172.
6. Ibid., 172.
7. Ibid., 173.
8. Phillips, *Running with Bonnie and Clyde,* 225.
9. Ibid., 225.
10. Ibid., 226.
11. Jim Patterson interview with prison officials, Texas prison records.
12. Texas prison records of Austin Avers.
13. Underwood, *Depression Desperado,* 124.
14. Kennedy interview, July 30, 1999.
15. Minutes of the Sixty-Eighth Meeting of the Texas Prison Board, Lee
Simmons testimony.
16. Minutes of the Sixty-Eighth Meeting of the Texas Prison Board, Simmons testimony.
17. Underwood, *Depression Desperado,* 124.
18. Minutes of the Sixty-Eighth Meeting of the Texas Prison Board, W. W.
Waid testimony.
19. Ibid., Waid testimony.
20. Ibid.
21. Ibid., Simmons testimony.
22. Phillips, *Running with Bonnie and Clyde,* 227.

23. Minutes of the Sixty-Eighth Meeting of the Texas Prison Board, Simmons testimony.
24. Underwood, *Depression Desperado*, 124.
25. Ibid., 228.
26. Minutes of the Sixty-Eighth Meeting of the Texas Prison Board, W. G McConnell testimony.
27. Ibid., Simmons testimony.
28. Kennedy interview, 30 July 1999.
29. Underwood, *Depression Desperado*, 228.
30. Minutes of the Sixty-Eighth Meeting of the Texas Prison Board, C. E. Burdeaux testimony.
31. Phillips, *Running with Bonnie and Clyde*, 228.
32. Underwood, *Depression Desperado*, 124.
33. Ibid., 124-125.
34. Mary Carey, interview with author. Carey is Roy King's ex-wife.
35. There are other reports saying that Walker had a rifle shot to the head. Although dramatic, this is untrue. The prison records are quite specific: "This date I find that the cause of death, according to the testimony of Lynn Hilbun, M.D., prison physician, was a gunshot wound to the chest. R. J. Camp, Justice of the Peace, Precinct 1, Walker County, Texas.
Physician's report on Whitey Walker, Texas prison records.
36. Minutes of the Sixty-Eighth Meeting of the Texas Prison Board, Waid testimony.
37. Special escape report on Whitey Walker, Texas prison records.
38. Minutes of the Sixty-Eighth Meeting of the Texas Prison Board, Simmons testimony.
39. Ibid., D. W. Roberts testimony.
40. Ibid., Roberts testimony.
41. Ibid., Waid testimony.
42. Phillips, *Running with Bonnie and Clyde*, 228-229.
43. Ibid., 230.
44. Ibid., 229.
45. Minutes of the Sixty-Eighth Meeting of the Texas Prison Board, Simmons testimony.
46. Phillips, *Running with Bonnie and Clyde*, 226-230.
47. Minutes of the Sixty-Eighth Meeting of the Texas Prison Board, Simmons testimony.
48. Simmons, Assignment Huntsville, 155-158.
49. Ibid.
50. Ibid.
51. Ibid.
52. Ibid.
53. Ibid.

CHAPTER 14: THE AFTERMATH
1. *Fort Worth Star Telegram*, 5 September 1976.
2. Simmons, *Assignment Huntsville: Memoirs of a Texas Prison Official*, 159.
3. Phillips, *Running with Bonnie and Clyde*, 231.

4. Phillips, *Running with Bonnie and Clyde*, 231.
5. Russell, unpublished manuscript, 12-13.
6. Simmons, *Assignment Huntsville: Memoirs of a Texas Prison Official*, 159.
7. Ibid., 160.
8. Ibid., 160.
9. Phillips, *Running with Bonnie and Clyde*, 275.
10. Ibid., 276.
11. Ibid., 277.
12. Ibid., 277.
13. Ibid.
14. *Amarillo Daily News*, December 8, 1934.
15. Ibid.
16. Day, *Captain Clint Peoples, Texas Ranger: Fifty Years a Lawman*, 38.
17. *Amarillo Daily News*, December 8, 1934.
18. Ibid.
19. Day, *Captain Clint Peoples, Texas Ranger: Fifty Years a Lawman*, 38-39.
20. *Amarillo Daily News*, 8 December 1934.
21. Ibid.
22. Ibid.
23. Ibid.
24. Phillips, *Running with Bonnie and Clyde*, 231.
25. *Amarillo Daily News*, December 8, 1934.
26. Ibid.
27. Ford interview, July 8, 1999.
28. Ibid.
29. Ibid.
30. Ibid.
31. Simmons, *Assignment Huntsville: Memoirs of a Texas Prison Official*, 161.
32. Ibid., 162.
33. Ibid., 161.
34. Phillips, *Running with Bonnie and Clyde*, 293.
35. Underwood, *Depression Desperado*, 205.
36. Phillips, *Running with Bonnie and Clyde*, 307.
37. Russell, unpublished manuscript, 16.
38. Ibid., 17.
39. Phillips, *Running with Bonnie and Clyde*, 294-295.
40. Ibid., 295.
41. Ibid., 295
42. Ibid., 296.
43. Byrd interview. Huntsville, Texas. 1999.

EPILOGUE: SUNDAY MORNING WITH THE WARDEN
1. Warden Jim Willett, interview with author, April 26, 1999.

Bibliography

BOOKS AND ARTICLES

Day, James M. *Captain Clint Peoples, Texas Ranger: Fifty Years a Lawman.* Waco, Texas: Texian Press, 1980.

Hamilton, George. "Lawman and Outlaws," in *Brazos County History: Rich Past —Bright Future*, ed. Glenna Fourman Brundidge. Bryan, Texas: Family History Foundation, 1986.

Lane, Eloise. "The Day They Robbed the Bank in Pampa." *Focus*, Summer 1989.

Phillips, John Neal. *Running with Bonnie and Clyde.* Norman, Okla.: University of Oklahoma, 1996.

Simmons, Lee. *Assignment Huntsville: Memoirs of a Texas Prison Official.* Austin, Texas: University of Texas Press, 1957.

Sinise, Jerry. *Black Gold and Red Lights.* Burnet, Texas: Eakin Press, 1982.

Tattersall, Peter D. *Conviction.* Pegasus Rex Press, 1980.

Thornton, Sue Bonner. *The Bonner Family History.* Waco, Texas: Texian Press, 1972.

Underwood, Sid. *Depression Desperado.* Austin, Texas: Eakin Press, 1995.

PUBLIC DOCUMENTS

District Court of Limestone County, Texas records, 87th Judicial District, May–June term, 1929.

James Mullins interview with prison officials June 3, 1938.

Minutes of the Sixty-Eighth Meeting of the Texas Prison Board. Huntsville, Texas, 24 July 1934.

Mullins' prison interview statement, Texas prison records.

Oklahoma prison records.

Jim Patterson interview with prison officials, Texas prison records.

Physician's report on Whitey Walker, Texas prison records.

Refugio County records, no. 831, Henry Methvin, judge's instructions to the jury.

Special escape report on Whitey Walker, Texas prison records.
The State of Texas v. Hilton Bybee, Cause No. 1690.
The State of Texas v. Irvin (Blackie) Thompson, Cause No. 1595, District Court of
    Falls County, Texas, 82nd Judicial District, Marlin, Texas, 28 June 1934.
The State of Texas v. Joe Palmer.
Texas prison records.
Texas prison records of Roy Johnson.
Texas prison records, Roy's side of the story.
Texas prison records, French's statement of events to prison officials.
Texas prison records of Austin Avers.

AUTHOR INTERVIEWS

Bauske, Joe. 22 May 1999.
Byrd, Pat.
Doerge, Mable. 8 October 1998.
Fling, Sam. 6 October 1998.
Ford, W. J.
Kennedy, Hugh. 30 July 1999.
McDonald, Jr., Judge Tom. 12 March 1999.
Palmer, Martha.
Rogers, Max.
Willett, Warden Jim. 26 April 1999.

NEWSPAPERS

Amarillo Daily News (Texas).
The Bryan Daily Eagle (Texas).
Fort Worth Star Telegram (Texas).
Marlin Daily Democrat (Texas).
Palestine Herald (Texas).
Temple Daily Telegram (Texas).

UNPUBLISHED PAPERS

Barner, S. E. "Hell-Bent Joe Palmer." True Detective Mysteries. Superinten-
    dent of Printing in the Texas Prison System.
Russell, Bud. "I Will Meet You in Hell."

Index

191

About the Author

Patrick M. McConal has been involved in speech communication since 1977, with an emphasis on public speaking regarding policy issues. He has been employed for fifteen years with the Texas Transportation Institute, where he currently serves as publications coordinator.

Mr. McConal holds a bachelor's degree in speech communication from Texas A&M University and an associate of arts degree from Blinn Junior College. He is also pursuing a master's degree in history at Sam Houston State University in Huntsville, Texas.

Over the Wall grew out of the author's graduate research and writing, as he specializes in Texas and outlaw history. He was preparing a paper on a local robbery when a search unearthed court transcripts hidden in a warehouse of the Court of Criminal Appeals in Austin, Texas. Those documents formed the basis for this book.

Patrick McConal lives in Bryan, Texas, with his wife, Pamela, their daughter, Maegan, and their sons Morgan and Brady. This is his first book.

Walker family photo near turn of the century.
Top left to right: Willie, Louis, Tom, unknown, John Middleton Walker,
Fannie, Sallie Mills Walker, Hugh, Ruth, Bryan.
— From the photo album of Nettie Walker,
courtesy of her granddaughter, Beth Walker Shipman

From left to right: Whitey Walker, Hugh Walker, unknown friend.
— Courtesy Sandra Walker

Hugh Walker (center) before a World War I battle.
—Courtesy Sandra Walker

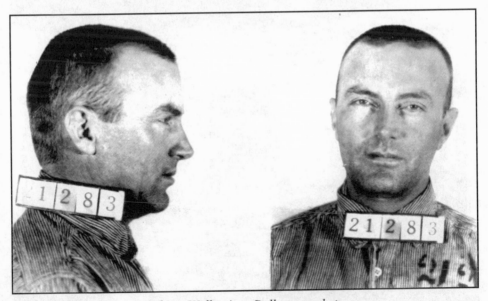

Whitey Walker in a Dallas mug shot.
— From the collections of the Texas/Dallas History
and Archives Division, Dallas Public Library

The First National Bank in Pampa before the robbery.
— Courtesy Eloise Lane

Teller cage at the bank. At one time, there were three cages.
— Courtesy Eloise Lane

Signal Hill today.

—Courtesy Eloise Lane

RAZOR
Owned by Ace Pendleton, who robbed the First National Bank, March 31, 1927. He later gave the razor to Rufe Jordan. Sheriff Jordan kept the razor for 64 years.

Razor that Ace Pendelton gave to Rufe Jordan.

— White Deer Land Museum

Roy A. JOHNSON Okla.Prison #15845 FP. 5/ 1 Aa 3
   aliases: 1 aA2a 2
R. A. GREGGERY, C. W. WARD, Homer WATT,Roy SEXTON.
Blk Hair; Bro.Eyes: 5-11-1/2: 172# 19-1925.
Mod. Build: Mod-Dk. Comp: Occ: Ball Player.
Res: Medford, Okla.
 10-29-33 Wanted by Sheriff, Palestine, Texas, and
Burn's Intl. Detect. Agy., Houston, Texas, for Robbery by Firearms. (Held up Robinson State Bank and
Trust Co., Palestine, Tex. on 10-26-33; tied up
employees, after making them open vault; secured
$4114.00 in cash and securities) May be in any of
the following cars.
1933 Ford V-8, Standard Coupe, Black with black wire
       Wheels, Tex. Lic. #4177, Mtr. #444749
1933 Ford V-8, Standard Sedan, Blue, with black wire
       Wheels, Tex. Lic. #4150, Mtr. 452145
1933 Ford V-8, Maroon Color Sedan, Tex. Lic.#585374
1933 Ford V-8, Coach, Grey Color, Tex. Lic. #465573

Roy Johnson mug shot and partial rap sheet.
—Bryan Public Library

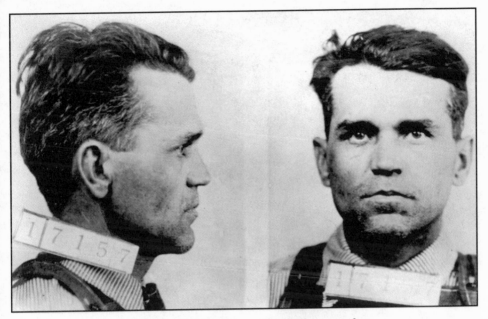

Irvin "Blackie" Thompson in a Dallas mug shot.
— From the collections of the Texas/Dallas History
and Archives Division, Dallas Public Library

*Left to right: Blackie's father William Thompson, Blackie's brother Frank, his
mother Pearl, Blackie, his sister Ethyle, brother Maurice, brother Cecil, and
brother George. Taken in June 1919 in Oklahoma at a funeral.*
— Courtesy W. S. Ford

Barber shop in Rogers, Texas, around 1920.
— Courtesy Violet Dolehite

Scene near Buckholts State Bank. Taller boy in background is Joe Zajicek.
— Courtesy Mr. and Mrs. Doyle Arnold

Joe Zajicek started his chase of the Whitey Walker Gang from this building, across the street from the bank.

Robinson State Bank and Trust Company, downtown Palestine.
— Courtesy Museum for East Texas Culture

Train depot at Palestine.
— Courtesy Museum for East Texas Culture

Downtown Bryan in 1910.
—Courtesy Bryan Public Library

Mrs. W. J. (Whitey) WALKER
    alias: Mrs. HAMM, Mrs. HELM.
Dark Hair: Dark Eyes: About 5-5, About 110 Lbs.
30 to 35 Years of Age. Med. Dark Complexion. Is
wife of W. J. Walker, Okla. State Prison 21283.
    Alleged to be implicated in series of Bank Rob-
beries, with Husband, and Roy A. JOHNSON, Okla.
Prison #15845 and Irvin THOMPSON, Okla. Prison 17157.
    This woman rents houses, etc. in towns where
robberies are "pulled"; renting houses in the fashion
able parts of the city. If you are able to identify
this woman or locate any record on her, kindly advise
the Wm. J. Burn's Intl. Detect. Agy., Houston, Texas.

Rare photo of Dolores Walker and partial rap sheet.
—Courtesy Bryan Public Library

Caldwell Jewelry in 1907.
—Courtesy Bryan Public Library

Marlin bath house in 1919. Sanitariums contributed to the town's wealth, which in turn attracted criminals.

—Courtesy Robert Mousner

Outside vault door of the First State Bank in Marlin.

Ventilation hole that V. M. Bradshaw looked through from his office into the vault.

*General area near Val Verde roadside where Walker hostages were kept
and tied with copper wire.*

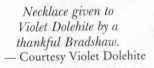

*Necklace given to
Violet Dolehite by a
thankful Bradshaw.*
— Courtesy Violet Dolehite

Sam Dolehite
— Courtesy Violet Dolehite

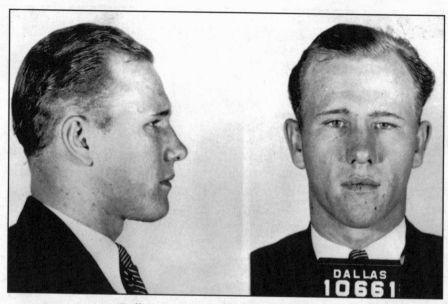

Dallas mug shot of Raymond Hamilton.
— From the collection of the Texas/Dallas History
and Archives Division, Dallas Public Library

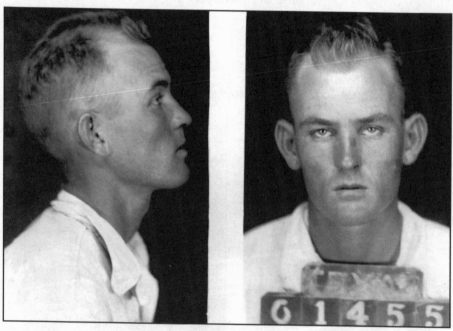

Dallas mug shot of Joe Palmer
— From the collection of the Texas/Dallas History
and Archives Division, Dallas Public Library

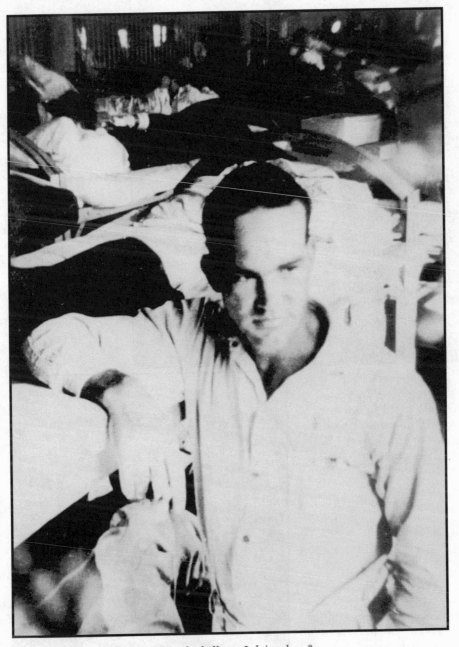

What the hell am I doing here?
This is one of several photos smuggled from three prisons
by Hugh Kennedy.

— Courtesy Hugh Kennedy

*Boss man overlooking
Hugh Kennedy in plow squad.
Kennedy bribed guards to
process the film and bring it
back to him, between
1934 and 1943.*
— Courtesy Hugh Kennedy

*Hoe squad. Prison stripes are for
escapees and parole violators.*
— Courtesy Hugh Kennedy

Kennedy with his plow squad mules. A palm camera was used by Kennedy and his friends to take these shots. The technique was to spread the fingers, point, and press.
— Courtesy Hugh Kennedy

Old Eastham as it stands today, a gutted warehouse.

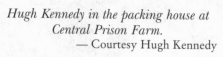

Hugh Kennedy in the packing house at Central Prison Farm.
— Courtesy Hugh Kennedy

Chow time in the fields.
— Courtesy Hugh Kennedy